LEADER

Devdutt Pattanaik writes, illustrates and lectures on the relevance of mythology in modern times. He has, since 1996, written over thirty books and 700 columns on how stories, symbols and rituals construct the subjective truth (myths) of ancient and modern cultures around the world. His books include *7 Secrets of Hindu Calendar Art* (Westland), *Myth=Mithya: A Handbook of Hindu Mythology* (Penguin Random House), *Jaya: An Illustrated Retelling of the Mahabharata* (Penguin Random House), *Sita: An Illustrated Retelling of the Ramayana* (Penguin Random House), *Olympus: An Indian Retelling of the Greek Myths* (Penguin Random House), *Business Sutra: A Very Indian Approach to Management* (Aleph Book Company), *My Gita* (Rupa Publications) and *Devlok with Devdutt Pattanaik* (Penguin Random House). To know more, visit devdutt.com.

LEADER

50 INSIGHTS FROM MYTHOLOGY

Devdutt Pattanaik

Illustrations by the author

HARPER
BUSINESS

Indus Source Books
Indian Spirit, Universal Wisdom

First published in 2006 by Indus Source Books

This revised and updated edition
co-published in hardback in India in 2017 by Harper Business
An imprint of HarperCollins *Publishers*
A-75, Sector 57, Noida, Uttar Pradesh 201301, India
www.harpercollins.co.in
and
Indus Source Books

2 4 6 8 10 9 7 5 3

P-ISBN: 978-93-5264-495-7
E-ISBN: 978-93-5264-496-4

Indus Source Books
PO Box 6194
Malabar Hill PO
Mumbai 400006
www.indussource.com

Typeset in Garamond by Special Effects, Mumbai

Printed and bound at
Thomson Press (India) Ltd

Within infinite myths lies an eternal truth
But who sees it all?
Varuna has but a thousand eyes
Indra has a hundred
You and I, only two

Contents

1	Becoming a leader	1
2	Tongue in court	5
3	Dreamers and implementers	9
4	Uneasy lies the head	13
5	Win, or be right?	19
6	The point of it all	25
7	Breaking the rules	31
8	Law of fishes	37
9	Churning out Lakshmi	43
10	Deeds for leaders	49
11	Kurukshetra counsel	55
12	The Vishwaroopa complex	59
13	Waiting to exile	65
14	The laws of the jungle	71
15	Common corporate culture beyond belief	77
16	Eyes of a leader	81
17	Strategic intent of Ravana	87
18	Vikramaditya and Vetal	93
19	Lever of charity	97
20	Proactive Garuda	103
21	The legacy lake	107
22	Throne of generosity	111
23	Binding tenacity	117
24	The poison of stagnation	121
25	The ultimate alpha male	125

26	Talking matters	129
27	Narada on the prowl	135
28	Different drum	141
29	Monkey leaders and cat leaders	147
30	When nobody cares	151
31	The palki	155
32	Wooing the right way	159
33	Both sides of the fence	165
34	Curse of kingship	169
35	Silent whispers	173
36	Implied needs	177
37	They don't have to think like you	181
38	Packaging matters	185
39	Challenging loyalty	189
40	Children of the blind	193
41	The weak in the pack	197
42	Law-abiding professionals	201
43	Rejection of the rest	205
44	Masculine and feminine leaders	209
45	Competitors and collaborators	213
46	The auditor's tragedy	217
47	Wrapped in rhythms	221
48	Unable to plan	225
49	Submit to regenerate	229
50	Recruitment dilemma	233

1

Becoming a leader

 When commenting on the great Indian epic, the Mahabharata, people often point to the question raised by Draupadi: Does a man who has gambled himself away have the right to gamble away his wife? But very few have asked: Does a king have the right to gamble away his kingdom? What gives the Pandavas, in general, and Yudhishthira, in particular, the right to gamble away his kingdom? A king is not the owner of the kingdom; he is its custodian.

If the kingdom is a cow that gives milk, the king is the cowherd. That is the traditional model of a leader in Hindu mythology. The king takes care of the kingdom and the kingdom nourishes him. He defends the kingdom and the kingdom empowers him. A cowherd cannot exist without a cow and a cow isn't safe without a cowherd. It's a symbiotic relationship. This is the essence of a king's role: to protect the cow, help it produce more calves, enable her to multiply and thrive, and in the process create more cowherds. This is growth—growth for the cow and growth for the cowherd.

In the Mahabharata, there is a great debate on who should be king. Should kingship be determined by bloodline or meritocracy? After much debate and discussion, and violence, which even involves an assassination attempt on the Pandavas, it is decided to divide the lands. The Pandavas get the underdeveloped half called Khandavaprastha, while their cousins, the Kauravas, get the prosperous city of Hastinapur. With the help of Krishna, the Pandavas transform Khandavaprastha into a great city called Indraprastha, which becomes the envy of the world. With the help of Krishna, the Pandavas even become kings. But then, Krishna leaves, and in his absence they gamble the kingdom away. It is almost as if, while they have the capacity to be king, they lack the attitude of kingship.

And so, Krishna offers them no reprieve when they have to suffer twelve years of exile in the forest, living in abject poverty, followed by a year of humiliation when the former kings live in hiding as servants in another king's palace. During this time there are tales of how each brother gets a lesson in humility and patience. In one episode, the brothers reach a lake where a heron warns them against drinking the water until they answer its question; the impatient Pandavas drink nevertheless and die, all except Yudhishthira. Yudhishthira pauses, answers the question, and is then allowed to drink. This displays a shift in character. The man, who, without thinking, gambled away his kingdom, is now ready to pause and think and question his actions and listen to good counsel before taking an action. He is suddenly more patient and prudent.

The heron then tells Yudhishthira that only one of his brothers will be brought back from the dead. He is asked to choose. 'Save Nakula,' he says. 'Why a weak stepbrother,' asks the heron, 'when you might as well save a strong brother like Bhima or a skilled one like Arjuna?' To this Yudhishthira says, 'My father had two wives. I, the son of his first wife, Kunti, am alive. Let one son of the second wife, Madri, live too.' Here again we see a transformation. Nakula was the first of the five brothers to be gambled away in the game of dice. Thus, the unwanted stepbrother, who mattered least in the gambling hall, matters most in the forest. Yudhishthira has learnt the lessons of Raj-dharma, that it is not due to his greatness and grandeur that the crown is placed on his head. He exists for others; he exists for the weakest in his kingdom; he exists to help the helpless. Otherwise, his kingdom is no different from the jungle where might is right. Otherwise, he is no different from an alpha male.

Krishna, the supreme divine cowherd, thus acts as a coach in the Mahabharata. He is not king as in his previous life of Rama (whose story is told in the Ramayana). Here he plays lowly roles as cowherd and charioteer, but acts as a kingmaker. He knows that it is not just about skill alone (turning the wilderness into a rich kingdom). It is about attitude. And to shift attitude, sometimes, one has to be dragged through misery—thirteen years of forest exile.

2

Tongue in court

The Bible tells the tale of the prophet, Nathan, who sought justice from his king, David, for a poor man who had been wronged by a rich man. Rather than taking one from his own flock to feed a traveller, the rich man claimed the one lamb that the poor neighbour dearly loved. David was understandably upset when he heard the complaint. He decreed that the rich man should die. No sooner did he take this decision than Nathan revealed that the rich man in his story was none other than David, a king with many wives. The poor neighbour was the Hittite, Uriah, with whose only wife, Bathsheba, the king had had an adulterous affair. By using the parable, Nathan had tricked the king into judging himself. He had made the king realize his own hypocrisy: quick to judge others but not himself.

Why did Nathan not simply tell the king that his actions were wrong? Would the king have heard him? Maybe he would have denied the crime, or simply made excuses for it. Despite being a representative of God, the prophet was wary of the king's ego and anger. And so he used the Trojan Horse method to address the sensitive issue.

The ability to communicate with a king with deference and dexterity is known in Sanskrit as Sabha-chaturya, which literally translated means 'tactfulness-in-court'. It is a trait that ministers and courtiers had to possess if they wished to survive in court and get their jobs done. It is a trait that people who work with leaders must possess. It is a trait that even leaders need to possess if they wish to lead.

The foundation for this skill lies in the observation that people are uncomfortable with the truth, especially when it shows them in a bad light or has consequences that could affect them adversely. When confronted with it, they react negatively—with rage or denial. They may get defensive or simply reject the submission. So the work does not get done. One needs strategic communication. One needs Sabha-chaturya.

Rathodji mastered the art of Sabha-chaturya long ago. He knew his boss, Khilachand, was a brilliant man with a rags-to-riches story. He also knew his boss had an ego the size of a mountain. He refused to accept or admit a mistake. In fact, if a mistake was pointed out, he would do everything in his power to justify it and stick to his guns. Khilachand was very fond of a distant cousin. So when a candidate presented himself before Khilachand with the cousin's recommendation, he was, without much consideration, appointed manager in one of the many oil depots he owned.

The candidate was a good-for-nothing fellow. He did no work and this caused a great deal of problems in the smooth running of operations. But no one dared tell this to Khilachand. To do so would mean that Khilachand was a fool to appoint a candidate purely on recommendation without checking credentials. And Khilachand did not appreciate being taken for a fool. In rage, just to prove he was right and everyone else who thought he was a fool was wrong, he would simply sack the guy who complained and give the candidate a raise and maybe even a promotion. It was irrational, but that's the way he was. Rathodji knew this and so, when the problem was presented to him, he pondered long and hard on how to give Khilachand the message without upsetting him and making matters worse.

The next day Khilachand and Rathodji had a long session gossiping about Khilachand's arch-rival, Mathias. Rathodji told Khilachand how Mathias had foolishly selected a candidate on his sister's recommendation and how the workers under the candidate were grumbling and planning to leave that firm and join their firm. Just while leaving, Rathodji gave Khilachand a file containing the new figures on operational efficiency with Khilachand.

The next day, Khilachand commented, 'I feel it is time to get the new candidate to work in the head office. What do you think?' Rathodji agreed. Sabha-chaturya had worked its magic. The message had been passed. No feathers were ruffled. The dignity of all parties was maintained. A profitable decision was made and all was well.

3

Dreamers and implementers

In Indian folklore, there are four characters. There is Shekchilli. There is Gangu Teli. There is Mitti ka Madhav (some say Gobar ka Ganesh) and there is Raja Bhoj. They most aptly describe the kind of people we have in our organizations.

Shekchilli is a dreamer. One day he gets a pot of milk from his master. He dreams of turning the milk into curd, then churning it for butter and selling the butter and making some money, and using that money to buy more milk and make more butter. And in time, making and selling so much butter that he would not have to work. As he dreams of the possibilities, he stumbles and falls on the road. The pot of milk in his hand breaks and out pours all the milk on to the ground.

Gangu Teli does not dream at all. He likes to implement things. He calls himself a 'realist' and focuses on practical things like doing the task and measuring its effectiveness and efficiency. That's what the world should be doing. He has a disdain for dreamers. His name Teli suggests that he is an oil presser. Just as an oil presser uses force to push oil out of oilseeds, Gangu Teli uses pressure to get work out of his team. Carrots, he says, are dreams; sticks, he insists, are reality. The story goes that when the wall of the king's fort on the mountain kept collapsing, the astrologer recommended the sacrifice of a woman and her newborn to appease the gods of the mountain. The only person whose wife and child were available for sacrifice—either voluntarily or under pressure, we will never know—was Gangu Teli. He is the front-line warrior; he knows. When times are bad, he will be called upon to make the ultimate sacrifice. The buck stops with him as he stands in the market. He is therefore most valued in the immediate term. Since he knows that, he often suffers from an inflated self-importance.

Mitti ka Madhav (also known by some as Gobar ka Ganesh) is neither a dreamer like Shekchilli nor an implementer like Gangu Teli. He is what you want him to be. On his own, he is neither. He is a reactive member of the team, doing whatever pleases you, with no mind or opinion of his own.

That brings us to Raja Bhoj, the ideal leader, a dreamer as well as implementer. If a 2×2 matrix of dreamers and implementers is created, Raja Bhoj sits in the top right-hand box while Mitti ka Madhav sits on the bottom left-hand box. Raja Bhoj knows when it is time to dream and when it is time to implement.

Pyne realized, to his horror, that his organization was full of Gangu Telis and Mitti ka Madhavs, when the recession hit. And he had to admit that it was his own fault. For six years the going was good. The demand for the copper pipes he made was greater than the supply. So he hired a number of executives who thought tactically and could sell. 'No dreamers for me,' he told his HR department, 'I want people who implement.' Pyne had had his experience with dreamers. They sat all day, made presentations to him, never moved out of air-conditioned offices, and imagined the market. He had to pay them a fat salary and there was no output of theirs that he could implement or measure. It was a waste of time. 'All this strategy nonsense is good for other companies. Not for me,' he said. So he created an organization where it was all about tasks and measurements. No creativity was celebrated. 'Let's just copy what the competitor does,' he said. 'Why waste time thinking?' Things went well for a long time. Growth in quarter after quarter. Bigger offices, more people, more sales, and good profits. Then came the recession.

All the businesses showed a fall in growth suddenly. No one wanted the copper pipes. Pipes sold were being returned. Payments were not being made. The salesmen were frustrated. Everyone shrugged their shoulders helplessly and hung their heads in shame. Pyne looked around and realized there was no idea he could copy to get out of the situation. Everyone was in the same boat. Almost everyone. There was one small company, belonging to one Raut, which was doing reasonably well. Their salesmen were not complaining and no one in his team feared losing a job. Pyne called on Raut, and Raut was kind to share his secret. 'You see, when the going was good, I imagined a time when things would not be so. Every boom is followed by a bust. So I created a small team to imagine a situation where there is no demand for copper pipes. How would we survive then? They came up with many ideas and I invested a small proportion of my profits to experiment with them. Most of them failed. But two ideas that they came up with are proving to be viable in these trying times.'

Pyne realized that Raut was a Raja Bhoj who had created a team of Shekchillis. Together they had dreamt of bust even in boom times. And this had enabled them to survive the bust. If only he had functioned like that! But then, he was no Raja Bhoj. He had taken pride in being Gangu Teli and now that the fort had collapsed, it was time for him to make the dreaded sacrifice of all that he dearly loved.

4

Uneasy lies the head

A few weeks ago, Jacob was asked by his boss to fire an incompetent employee who had been with the firm for two years. Jacob knew the decision was justified: despite repeated warnings the gentleman had refused to improve. He kept coming late to office, making excuses, leaving his work half done, refusing to admit there was a problem that needed addressing. But firing him? Was there no other option? The boss said, 'The decision has been taken after due consideration. There is no going back. All I want you to do is communicate the news to him.' 'Why me?' asked Jacob. No answer was given. Jacob just had to do it.

That was the worst task Jacob had ever done. When he was made department head, he had not been told that firing people would be part of the job. Suddenly, the job did not seem as glamorous and exciting as he had hoped it would be. He now realized the meaning of the phrase, 'Heavy is the head that wears the crown.' For nights he was haunted by images of the man breaking down when he was told he had to pack up and leave in seven days and that he would be paid two months' salary to help him while he looked for another job. Jacob had to listen to all those piteous pleas, all those requests for one last chance, with a stony face. It was simply horrible. He hated his boss for making him go through this.

Now Jacob was asked to do something else. He was given a junior staff member, who had joined the organization roughly eight months ago and was declared by another manager to be totally incompetent. The boss said, 'I give you two months to turn this boy around.' 'Why can't we just fire him?' Jacob asked. No answer was given. He just had to do it.

Jacob is not sure he is capable of this. But then, he had not thought he was capable of terminating another man's employment. He had somehow found the strength to do so. Now he was being asked to do the very opposite. He was being asked to sustain another man's employment and develop his competencies. Could he do that? A little voice in Jacob's heart told him he could.

Jacob's boss is doing what Rishi Vishwamitra did to Rama in the Ramayana. In the Ramayana, after Rama completes his education under Rishi Vashishtha, Vishwamitra storms into Dasharatha's court and demands that Rama accompany him to the forest and protect his hermitage from the rakshasas. Dasharatha offers his army instead because Rama is just a boy. 'No, I want Rama,' snarls Vishwamitra. With great reluctance, Dasharatha lets Rama go.

In the forest, Vishwamitra first directs Rama to shoot and kill the rakshasa woman, Tadaka. 'But she is a woman,' says Rama, remembering his lessons that informed him that women should never be harmed. Vishwamitra does not heed this argument. It does not matter that Tadaka is a woman; she threatens the well-being of the hermitage and does not heed warnings, hence she must be killed. Rama thus learns how all rules have to be contextualized. He therefore raises his bow and shoots Tadaka dead.

Later, Vishwamitra takes Rama to the hermitage of Rishi Gautama. There Rama is shown a rock which was once Gautama's wife, Ahalya. Her husband found her in the arms of another man, Indra, king of the gods, and so he cursed her to turn into a rock, explains Vishwamitra. Rama is then asked by the rishi to place his foot on the rock. That touch turns the rock back into Ahalya and she rises to the heavens, purified of all her sins. Rama realizes there are times when one has to strike and times when one has to forgive.

The killing of Tadaka and the rescue of Ahalya are two extreme events. One reeks of ruthlessness and the other brims with compassion. In one, there is death, in the other there is life. With these two events, Rama's practical education which began with theoretical education under Vashishtha is complete. By experiencing two extreme roles of a leader, Vishwamitra transforms the boy that is Rama into a man, one who is ready to take on the responsibility of leadership, one who is ready for marriage and kingship.

The education of Rama is the story of how leaders can

be made. It draws attention to the power of a leader and explains in what situation this power can be used to take life and in what situation the same power can be used to give life. It demonstrates how there are situations when a king is called upon to take a tough call and situations where the king is expected to be compassionate. This cannot be taught in a classroom; one has to live it. That is why Vishwamitra stormed into Dasharatha's court and took Rama into the forest by force.

Vishwamitra, one must remember, is not an ordinary sage. Unlike Vashishtha who is born a rishi, Vishwamitra was once a king who, through spiritual austerities, became a rishi. Thus he knows what a king is expected to do and what a king has to go through as he lives his role. That is why he insists on completing Rama's education and that is why Vashishtha does not stop him.

Jacob's boss is helping Jacob learn leadership. He could have fired the employee himself since the decision had already been taken. By making Jacob do what is considered to be one of the worst tasks in corporate life, he was making Jacob sensitive to the demands of a higher office. It is not just about power and perks; it is also about taking calls and accepting responsibility. But being boss is not just about having the power to fire people; it is also about developing the skill to train and retain people. This is what the boss is trying to do when he asks Jacob to mentor a junior staff member who has been written off by other managers.

Here is an opportunity for Jacob to save a life. Will Jacob do it? If he does, Jacob's boss will know that Jacob is a talent, one who has to be retained in the organization and groomed for leadership roles. If he does not, Jacob's boss will know that Jacob still has miles to go before he can even aspire to be king.

Win, or be right?

 learned sage was in the middle of a very narrow bridge when he saw a powerful king approaching from the other side. 'Please turn around,' said Shakti-muni, 'so that I may pass.'

'No, you turn around,' thundered the king, 'so that I may pass.'

'But I stepped on the bridge first.'

'Yes, but I can push you back.'

'That's not fair. Know that I am a teacher, a priest and the most respected philosopher in the land. Hence, I must be given the first right of passage,' argued the sage.

The king sneered, 'I built the school you teach. I pay for the rituals you perform. Without me as patron, you would not be able to indulge in philosophy. So you must give me the first right of passage.'

So the arguments continued, each one refusing to give way to the other, each one justifying why the other should turn back. Finally, the king raised his whip and struck the sage. Furious, the sage cursed the king, 'You have behaved like a demon, so may you turn into one.' Instantly, the king turned into a demon—a man-eating demon. He pounced on the sage, opened his mouth wide and ate him whole.

What mattered more: crossing the bridge or crossing the bridge first? Clearly the latter, for the sage. That is why, instead of simply turning back to make way for the bully king, he demanded first right of passage. The demand turned to insistence on moral, ethical and legal grounds. But what happened finally? The sage did not win the argument; he did not even get to cross the bridge. In the end, he was reduced to cannibal fodder. Sometimes in our obsession to be right, we lose sight of the goal and lose the game. What would have happened if he had allowed the king to pass? He would have been on the other side, alive, albeit a little late and with a dented ego. Would that have been so terrible? Though learned, the sage was not wise enough to realize that, in the long run, being right does not matter; winning does.

We often fall into the trap of 'wanting to be right'. Righteous indignation is a self-indulgent path, one that often distracts us from our destination. Somaraju realized this at the end of his quarterly business review.

Somaraju had not met his quarter's target. The market had not responded as expected. He knew he could make up, even surpass, the half-yearly target, provided he got an increase on his promo budget. He entered the review meeting with all facts and figures to explain his proposal. He knew he had a fight on his hands, especially since there were rumours that the MD planned to rationalize and cut down the total promo budget altogether so as to meet the bottom-line target.

The meeting began well. After the exchange of pleasantries, the PowerPoint presentation was beamed on the white screen. The graphs were shown, the numbers were discussed and the explanations were offered. Somaraju was clearly well prepared and he could see that the management was quite pleased with the way he was putting forth his case. Suddenly, the CFO said, 'I don't think you managed the hospital account well!'

Somaraju did not like this at all. The hospital account being referred to was an extremely difficult one to manage. And things had been made worse because the finance department had delayed some payments due to the party. 'I don't think so, sir,' said Somaraju sharply.

An argument followed, with the CFO explaining why he felt the hospital account was not managed well and Somaraju refuting all that was being said. The scene got quite ugly. The CFO started pointing to the lackadaisical attitudes displayed by some of the sales guys. Somaraju retorted by accusing the finance department of sitting in an ivory tower with no clue as to what was happening in the real world out there.

After about fifteen minutes, the MD had had enough. 'Can we get on with the presentation?' he asked. The CFO withdrew and Somaraju restarted. The energy had changed in the room. The focus was lost. Somaraju went into defensive overdrive, explaining how every client was managed well. He oversold his case and only succeeded in making more and more people see the CFO's point of view. By the end of the meeting, not only was Somaraju's promo budget cut, he got an impression that some of the management members felt he should be relieved of his portfolio. Somaraju returned to his cabin later that evening a dejected man. He even contemplated resigning.

What went wrong? The problem started when the CFO made a comment on hospital accounts. Somaraju had many options then: he could have agreed without being apologetic or defensive ('I know, sir, but please let me explain the situation'), or he could have respectfully disagreed ('I appreciate your opinion on the matter, but given the circumstances, I do believe our team has done a fairly good job'), or he could have enrolled the CFO ('I have been meaning to seek your advice on that account'), or he could have just side stepped it, smiling, not reacting, and simply proceeding with the presentation. Instead, he decided to confront the CFO. He got so allured by the desire to prove he was right that he forgot the reason he was in the meeting in the first place.

Sometimes, when one finds oneself on a narrow bridge with an opponent on the other side, it helps to ask what matters more—getting the other to turn around or getting oneself across the bridge.

Does this mean that to win one must never try to be right? No, it does not mean that. Winning is one thing, being right is another. We must not confuse issues. It is possible to win and be right. But when the choice is between winning and being right, one needs to choose wisely. More often than not, we prefer being right because it pampers the ego in the short term. In the long term, however, winning yields better results.

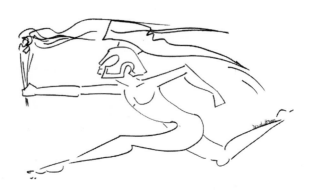

6

The point of it all

The Olympic motto '*Citius, Altius, Fortius*' is Latin for 'Swifter, Higher, Stronger'. The roots of this ideal of continuous relentless improvement lie in the ancient Greek world, where the Olympic Games were a sacred ritual. Through participation, and especially through winning, the athlete reached the 'zone' that brought him closer to the gods. That was the whole point of the games—to be better than what one was and break the assumed limitations imposed on man by the gods.

It is this ideal that governs businesses today and propels the desire to be bigger, grow faster, ride up the value chain. Our business models do have their roots in Western business practices which in turn have been shaped by ancient Greek ideals. Business leaders are heroes, like Ulysses and Hercules. They are expected to go where no one has gone before, on great solitary adventures, creating new markets, penetrating old ones, fighting the demons of opposition and emerging triumphant. The whole point of the game is to win—to outlast the competition, to rise above mediocrity, to create new horizons, to shatter old boundaries. Little wonder then that the Greek god of business and trade was Hermes, who had wings on his sandals, always on the run.

But why do we assume this to be the universal model? When Alexander came to India and said that he wanted to conquer the world, the local sages asked, 'Why?'

These sages must have been familiar with the Jain story of Bharata, who conquered the whole world and then ordered stone carvers to climb up the Mount Meru, the mountain in the centre of the world, and carve on its peak his name, declaring him the first one who conquered the world. The stone carvers climbed the mountain but returned soon after, their faces glum. 'We cannot do it, sir,' they said. 'Why?' asked Bharata. 'We cannot explain, go up and see for yourself.' Bharata climbed the mountain and when he reached the peak he found every inch of the peak covered with names of former kings, each one declaring, 'I too conquered the world.' Suddenly, Bharata realized the pointlessness of any achievement. The event forced him to sit back and reflect on life.

The same story is retold in Hindu mythology in a different way. Indra wanted Vishwakarma, his architect, to build him a palace befitting his stature as king of the gods. A great palace was built but Indra found it was not good enough. 'Make it bigger, grander,' said Indra. So another palace was built. Even that was not good enough. A frustrated Vishwakarma went to Vishnu who promised to sort things out. Vishnu approached Indra in the form of a boy and took a tour of the palace. 'Very good,' he said. 'Very good indeed, but not as good as that of the other Indra.' The remark intrigued Indra. 'What do you mean, the other Indra?' he asked the boy. And the boy explained, 'The Indras who existed before you. The Indras who will exist after you. The Indras who exist right now in other worlds.' And Indra said, 'What do you mean? Are there others like me?' And the boy said, 'Of course. Countless others.' Suddenly Indra felt small and insignificant in the grand cosmos. He was but a grain of sand on a beach of Indras. With this realization, his life became less about aspiration and more about introspection.

While Indians celebrated the cyclical nature of life, the Greeks despised the very idea. For the Greeks, hell was becoming Sisyphus who spent all day taking a rock up the mountain only to find that the rock had rolled down at night, forcing him to do today what he had done yesterday. Glory came when one broke free, did something different and new. This made man a hero and assured him a place in the Greek heaven of the Elysian Fields. Greeks broke free from the monotony of existence by achieving something spectacular in the material world itself. But for Indians, breaking free meant breaking free from the material world itself. Unlike the Greek world where the point of life was self-actualization, the point of life in the Indian world was self-realization. In India, the great question was never how you can be swifter, higher and stronger, but: why should you be swifter, higher and stronger. If introspection revealed that the point of one's actions was indulging the ego, one was a fool, further entrapping oneself in the mire of materialism. The wise man worked not to indulge the ego, but to triumph over it—and this happened when one truly and sincerely worked for others.

A business leader may argue that current business models are about others. That it is not (only) about ego and greed, it is also about creating jobs, democratizing wealth, and about survival. It is our responsibility to help more and more people live a better standard of life; hence we need to grow. And we must keep running ahead of the competition before they gain ground and overwhelm us. Both these viewpoints reaffirm that we are increasingly subscribing to the Greek way of thinking and less to the Indian way of thinking. No more is life a cycle, now it is a flat road where we are being chased by demons. If we run fast enough we will reach that wonderful place where there is no poverty, no strife, no competition. Such beliefs only bemuse Indian sages, for they believe you cannot change the cyclical world, only your viewpoint.

Is the Indian belief in fate and rebirth the reason why Indians are not so aggressive? Is that why Indians seem happy despite poverty? Is that why Indians are so comfortable bending the rules—how does it matter anyway? Is that why Indians are so tolerant of everything, even terrible infrastructure and bad governance? Is that a good thing? Do we want to change— become more Greek? Not passive sages but proactive heroes?

As the world gets smaller, we are being led to believe that

there is only one game to be played, with only one set of rules and one set of ideals. We are being asked to be swifter, higher and stronger. We are basking in the glory of young achievers and following the footsteps of global winners. But sometimes, maybe sometimes, we need to take time out from the Greek world and ask ourselves this very Indian question: Where from comes our ambition and where is it taking us? Maybe the answer will create a workplace that is less paranoid, less aggressive, less stressed and more at peace with itself. And that may not be so bad.

7

Breaking the rules

Two childhood friends, one the son of a warrior, the other the son of a priest, promised to share all they possessed even in adulthood. Fortune, however, favoured only the warrior's son. In desperation, the priest's son who had been reduced to abject poverty hesitantly decided to approach his rich friend. This story has two endings.

In the Mahabharata, the pauper Drona is insulted by his friend, Drupada, king of Panchal, for assuming that promises of childhood matter in adulthood. He is asked to beg for charity rather than demand a share of the royal fortune in the name of friendship. A furious Drona leaves the palace determined to become Drupada's equal—a decision that leads to a spiral of vendetta that culminates in the bloody carnage at Kurukshetra. In the *Bhagavata,* however, the pauper is Sudama and he is warmly welcomed and showered with lavish

gifts by his friend, Krishna. So how must a leader behave—
like Krishna or Drupada? The answer is not as simple as one
assumes.

Drupada is doing what a king is supposed to: laying down
the law, telling Drona not to curry personal favours, and
advising him instead to behave in keeping with his role in
society. As a priest, Drona can either ask for a fee (dakshina),
if services are rendered, or for charity (daan), if no services
are rendered. Drupada is doing the right thing. Unfortunately,
he does so rather nastily, without empathy. His actions do not
display the spirit of generosity and that is his undoing.

One often forgets why laws and rules and codes of conduct
exist. They exist to ensure fairness. If there were no laws,
anarchy would reign, might would be right, the meek would be
at the mercy of the strong, favouritism and nepotism would
breed, and only the fit would survive. Through laws, a leader
overpowers the law of the jungle and creates a space where
even the weak can thrive and grow to their fullest potential.
Laws ensure that the urge of the strong and the loud to
dominate is restrained so that the weakest can breed and the
meekest are heard. Thus the 'spirit of generosity' underlies
every 'rule of restraint'. At least, it is supposed to.

One manager in a public sector company believed in an
open door policy. Anybody could walk into his cabin any time
with any issue. This made him highly popular. But over time
he realized that this prevented him from giving people who
came to his room his full attention. There was always someone
entering the room, ignoring the one already in the room,

distracting him with some other agenda. So he put down a rule: meetings by appointment only. His popularity dipped, until everyone realized this policy ensured that all those who went to him got full attention in the time allotted to them.

The rule had ensured fairness—no single meeting dominated other meetings. Months passed. The appointment rule became rigid. No one could meet the manager without appointment, even if there was a crisis. The secretary started enjoying the power he got in defining who got to meet the boss, and when. He enjoyed reminding the boss that it was time for the next meeting.

Sometimes the manager really wanted to extend the meeting, but rules—his rules—were rules, and had to be respected. The manager started being perceived as a rigid man who lacked the personal touch, because somewhere along the line he forgot the purpose of his own rules. He had become Drupada. When rules do not generate fairness, it is time to bend them, or break them, as Krishna does repeatedly in the *Bhagavata* and the Mahabharata.

The story of Karna in the Mahabharata draws attention to how we often overlook the very principle that underlies laws. Karna was a generous man; anyone who came to his door never left empty-handed. And yet, he abandoned the spirit of generosity when it mattered most—when a helpless woman, being publicly disrobed by her own kinsmen, begged for help. The woman, Draupadi, ironically the daughter of Drupada, questioned the men about the appropriateness of their actions.

Everyone felt sorry for her, but not one of them raised a finger to help because everyone agreed no rule was actually broken: her husbands had gambled her away, she had been won fairly and her new masters had a right to treat their new property as they wished. Here was an opportunity to challenge the law, bend it, change it, appealing to humanity, so that the law served its primary purpose—to help the helpless, to reverse the law of the jungle.

Unfortunately, everyone, Karna included, hid behind the letter of the law and forgot its spirit. For this oversight, the gods never forgave Karna; taking advantage of his charitable nature, they stripped him of his divine armour and left him vulnerable in the battlefield of Kurukshetra.

Understanding the purpose of a law helps the leader bend it or change it as and when the situation demands it. A young executive wanted permission to leave his office early, at 4 p.m. instead of 5 p.m., so that he could attend his MBA classes at 6 p.m. In Drupada's world, this would not be allowed for fear that others would demand a similar flexibility. This would have only bred frustration and created an executive who would have spent all day looking at the clock and sprinting out whenever the clock struck five, leaving his work half done.

In Krishna's world, the executive would have perhaps been allowed to take leave at 4 p.m. without being asked to compensate for time. This would have created a very happy executive but also an organization where rules would never be respected. Luckily for Krishna, beside him sit his many wives, each one a form of Lakshmi. When he kept offering

Leader: 50 Insights from Mythology

Sudama gifts, they caught hold of his hand and said, 'Leave some for us,' reminding him that while generosity is fine, restraint is good too if one wants to run a household, and an organization.

In a world where Krishna rules and Lakshmi matters, the young executive would have been told why the rules of time were in place. A compromise would have been reached and the student would have been asked to compensate for the time lost by perhaps coming earlier to work or by working through lunch hour. This would have generated an enthusiastic and indebted employee, and not threatened organizational order. This is what the scriptures call a 'win-win' situation.

8

Law of fishes

The *Vishnu Purana* begins with the story of the Matsya avatar, the fish incarnation of Vishnu.

A tiny fish approaches Manu, the first leader of mankind, on the riverbank and begs him to save him from the big fish. Manu, in his compassion, scoops the tiny fish out of the river in the palm of his hand and puts it in a pot. The tiny fish is immensely grateful. But the next day the tiny fish has grown in size and the pot is too small to accommodate it. Manu transfers the fish to a big pot. A day later, the fish has grown once again. Manu has to move it to a giant pitcher. That too is not enough a day later. So the fish is moved from the pitcher to a pond, from the pond to a lake, from the lake to a river and finally the sea. Even the sea is not enough. So the rains start to fall and the ocean expands to make room for the fish. As the ocean expands, the waters creep over the earth and soon Manu realizes that the whole world will soon be submerged by the rising waters. The rain continues to fall and the sea continues to rise, making more and more room for the fish. Manu cries out in alarm and wonders what is happening. The fish smiles and transforms into Vishnu, and promises to save Manu from the flood. It asks Manu to take refuge in a boat for himself, his family, for various animals and plants, and for the seven wise sages in whose custody rests the wisdom of the world (the Hindu Noah's ark some may say). The giant fish then guides this boat through the rain and storm to the peak of Mount Meru, the only piece of land that survives the great flood of doom.

Why does Vishnu take the form of a fish for his first interaction with mankind? And what does this story have to do with the corporate world?

To understand this one must first understand the Sanskrit phrase 'matsya nyaya' which means 'law of the fishes', whose equivalent in English is the phrase 'law of the jungle'. In the story, the tiny fish asks Manu to save him from the big fish. But in nature, no one would come to the tiny fish's rescue because in the jungle everyone is on their own and only the fit survive. Manu, however, is human and not entirely part of nature. He has been given the faculty by which he can defy the law of the jungle. That is what makes a man a man. Manu acts, not from the need to survive, but out of compassion. The moment he scoops the fish out and saves it, civilization is born: a place where even the weakest can thrive. The laws instituted to make this happen are dharma, making matsya nyaya the very opposite—adharma.

A government is like Manu, trying to create through its laws and regulations a system where the weakest can thrive and the strong don't dominate the weak. They don't want large MNC and business houses (the big fish) to establish a monopoly and seize control of the market. They want the smaller players to thrive too. Hence, they impose regulations and licences and laws and do everything in their power to stamp out a market where anything goes. Such actions by the government destroying the 'free' market and stifling laissez-faire have been repeatedly denounced. But they are necessary, since man, while capable of extreme generosity, is also capable of extreme greed. Government laws and regulations and licences are needed to protect the interests of the weaker sections of society, to ensure a fair distribution of wealth.

The tiny fish, however, does not remain a tiny fish forever. It grows in size. Unable to provide for itself, totally dependent on Manu, it begs for more—a bigger pot, a bigger pond. And Manu, in his compassion, keeps giving and giving and giving, until finally even the sea is not big enough for the fish. Rains must come and the sea must expand so that the fish can be accommodated. In the process Manu's world is destroyed.

Thus the story shows the price of foolhardy compassion. Neither Manu nor the fish are willing to face a truth—that the fish is no longer helpless. Manu, because he is afraid of being seen as less compassionate. The fish, because it is afraid of fending for itself.

This has happened in India where laws and regulations and licences ended up stifling growth and destroying the economy. The rules had to be changed. The markets had to open up to foreign investments. Manu had to let the fish help itself. But that has not been taken kindly. Everywhere we see protests, riots and marches against the opening up of the Indian economy. The fish is afraid and is lashing out at Manu, which perhaps never prepared the fish for this moment.

A leader is like Manu. While creating more markets, he has to consciously sometimes invest disproportionately higher amounts in small developing markets over large developed ones. In the absence of such concerted effort, the budget can be totally appropriated by the big sales team managing the developed markets with its grand promises, leaving the small sales team with little or no budget. A good leader never asks the smaller markets for immediate returns. The bigger markets may cry foul and taunt the leader with proof that if more investments were made it could perhaps cough up a bigger return. But the leader's vision is long term. The big market may not be big forever and the small market will eventually grow. For the moment, the tiny fish needs its pot and pond, and the big fish can manage in the sea.

But a shrewd leader must be wary of the plan becoming a habit. The developing market can choose to call itself a developing market forever. It is possible that nobody has noticed that it is becoming a developed market, that it does not need that extra care it was given initially, that it now has the power to play with the big boys. A wise leader should

Leader: 50 Insights from Mythology

always keep an eye on the size of the fish and know when it is time to throw it back into the sea. Good leadership is about capacity building. A good leader is not someone who gives you the fish—he is one who teaches you how to fish. That is the first lesson of the *Vishnu Purana*.

9

Churning out Lakshmi

 The ultimate goal is profit. Call it anything you want: bottom-line, top-line, market share, capitalization, equity, dividends, incentive, or growth. It is what ultimately counts. It is why leaders are sought by organizations. Leaders are the ones who are able to mobilize the organizational resources to generate wealth. They are Vishnus engaged to churn out Lakshmi, the mythological embodiment of profit, from the ocean of milk. Lakshmi, the bejewelled goddess of wealth and fortune who sits on a lotus, is the most popular goddess in India. Her image can be found gracing most households and business establishments. Everybody wants her. Her footprint is often painted on doorways pointing inwards because everyone wants her to walk towards them. Leaders exist to make this happen.

Unfortunately, Lakshmi is Chanchala, the fickle one. Few

can predict where she plans to go. Sometimes her movements are predictable. Often they aren't, confounding the most astute of analysts. Exasperated by her whimsical ways, some have concluded that Lakshmi is cross-eyed—she looks one way but often moves the other. But there is one thing scriptures are sure of: Lakshmi will always move towards Vishnu. She is drawn to him. Vishnu is Shrinivas which means 'where Lakshmi resides'. He is Lakshmikanta—'beloved of Lakshmi'. What is it that he does that makes him attractive to fortune? If leaders can discover this, they too can become Vishnu; they too can become magnets of Lakshmi. In all of Vaishnava literature, Vishnu is never shown chasing Lakshmi. Two groups of minor deities chase Lakshmi. They are devas and asuras.

Asuras live under the earth and Lakshmi is addressed as Patala Nivasini, a resident of the subterranean region because the ancients realized long ago that wealth in its most primal form—minerals and plants—comes from under the ground. Asuras are deemed demons because they cling to Lakshmi and will not let her go. She is Paulomi, their daughter and their sister.

The devas who live above the ground as fire and wind and sun and sky have to fight to release Lakshmi. Observe how all primary wealth-generating activities are violent—the tilling of soil, the harvesting of crop, the threshing of grain, the smelting of metal. This 'value-generating violence' is described in mythology as the war of asuras and devas, the hoarders and distributors of wealth, the demons and the gods.

Leader: 50 Insights from Mythology

Devas transform Paulomi into Sachi, the consort of their king, Indra. But Indra, in his recklessness, knows to enjoy Sachi but not retain her—the fickle one moves away rapidly, leaving Indra's paradise shorn of all life and beauty. Indra begs his father, Brahma, to help, who in turn directs the gods to Vishnu, who advises them to take the help of the asuras, for only the asuras possess the magical 'Sanjivani vidya' that can regenerate what has been lost. Thus devas can draw, distribute and spend wealth, but they cannot create wealth.

Who are the devas of the corporate world? Could it be the flashy marketing and sales guys who go around getting the business, generating demand for products and services? In that case who are the asuras? Are they the product makers and the service providers? Can production/service exist without marketing/sales? Can the gods in the sky exist without demons on earth? No, they cannot. Vishnu, the leader, knows this and therefore sides with no one in particular. He knows that the two make up the force and counter-force that will churn Lakshmi out from the ocean of milk. The trick is the ability to balance the two sides of the team. A tilt one way or the other will be disastrous. It will cause the churn to collapse. Devas are guided by Brihaspati, god of the planet Jupiter, who in astrology is associated with logic, rationality and mathematics. The guru of the asuras is Shukra, god of the planet Venus, who in astrology is associated with emotion, creativity and intuition. Brihaspati's logical approach makes him balanced; he is therefore visualized as having two eyes, while Shukra, whose intuitive approach makes him imbalanced and unpredictable, is visualized as having one eye. Like the devas and asuras, even Brihaspati and Shukra are pitted against each other. It is the battle of logic and intuition.

The corporate world is full of Brihaspatis and Shukras, the logicians and the magicians. The former prefer excel sheets, the latter prefer PowerPoints. The former usually have a finance background, the latter are part of sales and marketing. People with a business school or science background are encouraged to become Brihaspatis but people with an arts background and in creative fields are encouraged to stay as Shukras. Brihaspatis are often preferred in corporate organizations because their language can be understood, controlled and predicted. Not so with Shukras. They are shunned until one realizes that survival depends on that wild and crazy out-of-the-box idea.

One can understand why devas led by Brihaspati are deemed 'gods': they live above the ground, are bathed in light, and are clear, transparent and logical, hence understandable. Asuras, led by Shukra, by contrast, live under the ground, are unseen; their intuition and creativity are unpredictable, unfathomable, uncontrollable, making them mysterious and magical. Asuras threaten us, make us insecure. Therefore they are demons. Please note that in Hindu mythology, unlike in Biblical mythology, demons are not evil creatures—Hindus have no Satan. They are children of Brahma just like devas. The divide between them is not moral or ethical. They are complementary forces of nature.

A true leader is able to harness the various forces around him to create an effective and efficient wealth-generating churn. He makes them complementary, not antagonistic. He works with both Brihaspati and Shukra, logic and magic, objectivity and subjectivity. He is able to get the best out of asuras and devas, product creators and value givers. He has sattva guna—the principle that balances the two other extreme principles: inertia/tamas of the asuras and the agitation/rajas of the devas. He is both rational on one hand and intuitive on the other. He respects flashy presentations but also knows the value of a robust excel sheet behind it. While doing all this, Vishnu never bothers with Laskhmi. He is almost indifferent to her. And that is why, perhaps, she chases him. She becomes his crown, his throne, his parasol and footstool. She makes him the king by serving as his profitable kingdom. One must be careful though. Lakshmi is not a faithful wife. Leaders often forget that success is drawn not to them but to their action. The crown follows the position, not the person. To keep Lakshmi walking towards them all the time, it is important that a leader always stays a Vishnu—always balanced, always focused, always impartial, and always detached.

10

Deeds for leaders

So it's your first day of work as the new leader of the team. Is it your appointment letter that makes you a leader? Or do actions make you a leader? What actions must you take to establish your leadership? Is there any step-by-step approach by which a leader can be made? While everyone agrees leaders are born, not made, scriptures do refer to a series of 'yagnas' or rituals that can make a king of a man.

The first of these is undoubtedly 'vivah' or marriage—marriage between the king and his kingdom, the leader and the organization. In epic times, a man could not be king without a queen by his side because the queen represented the kingdom. Just as a husband has to love, protect, nourish and delight his wife, the king was expected to love, protect, nourish and delight his kingdom.

This connection between the leader and the organization

is critical. He has to believe in the organization, its goals, and its values, or he cannot be a leader. In the absence of vivah, a man is not a leader, just an employee doing a job that gives him salary and status. Don't expect him to be proactive, creative or enthusiastic.

After vivah, Rajasuya yagna has to be performed. In the Mahabharata, when Yudhishthira expresses his desire to be a king, Krishna advises him to do something spectacular like killing the mighty Jarasandha before organizing the Rajasuya or coronation ceremony. 'Only then will they respect your kingship and acknowledge your sovereignty.' Before a man is promoted to a senior position, it is critical that he be accepted by his peer group—the other kings. To justify this rise, he needs some tangible achievement, a proof of concept, without which he remains a wannabe, a dreamer. In many tribes, for example, the future king was encouraged to kill a lion or tiger or wolf. Only this would make men follow him into a battle.

Part of the coronation ceremony involved 'abhishek', when in the presence of all, water was poured over the king. This 'public bathing' was a transformation ritual. It put a man on a pedestal, made him special, the first among equals, greater than the rest.

Often, and this is typically seen in sales companies, a field manager is sent to his headquarters without any attempt by the management to ceremonially crown him king in front of those he is supposed to manage. He lands up in the city alone and has to spend weeks asserting his managership.

The transition is not always smooth or successful. A simple

meeting or meal where the management introduces the manager formally to the executives who are supposed to follow him gives the manager a much-needed validation. It tells the team that the manager has the blessings of a 'higher power'.

After the crown has been publicly placed, a manager often faces hostility from his team. He is a stranger, a new boss. Relationships have to be established. Hierarchies and processes have to be put in place. The worst thing to do is to add value or impose authority without connecting with the team.

For this connection, an Upanishad is required—a discussion, a debate, a hearing of everyone's views before the leader declares his vision. This 'hearing' must be genuine. There are clever leaders who hear but never listen. This is soon discovered and the leader ends up losing the connection with the team.

After the Upanishad, the king had to define his dharma— his vision and how he expects this to be realized. Dharma had two components: varna or station in the organization and ashrama or stage of the employee. Varna-dharma means defining the roles, the rights and the responsibilities of every employee.

Often, this is never clarified. When roles overlap, there is chaos. The vision is forgotten and personal rivalries drive the organizational agenda. This can be seen as a measure of leadership failure. To lead, one must be clear what one wants and what each member of the team is supposed to do to make that happen.

Ashrama-dharma means knowing which member of the organization is in which stage of his job or his career—learning stage, delivering stage, teaching stage or retiring stage. If a person has outgrown his job, it is time to give him a new job. If a person has outgrown his responsibility, it is time to give him a higher responsibility. Otherwise he will wither away and sap the organization of its strength.

The most spectacular of royal yagnas in ancient times was the Ashwamedha, during which the royal horse wandered freely followed by the king's army. All the lands the horse traversed unchallenged became part of the king's dominion. Those who stopped the horse had to answer to the king's soldiers.

A king's Ashwamedha yagna helped identify those who submitted to him and those who challenged him. Ashwamedha was a dangerous ritual: it could lead to a king's defeat and humiliation. In the corporate world, there are no horses. But every leader has an agenda, a vision he seeks to realize.

This is his horse. The information, facts and arguments that he has to back his vision are his army. The PowerPoint presentation, one could say, is the horse; the excel sheet with all the research data justifying the numbers presented is the army. Without a strong army the horse will be challenged. To stay a leader, the horse must traverse unchallenged or the army must be strong enough to overpower any challenge.

Once the conquest is complete, and the idea has been planted in the organization, the king must do his Digvijaya yatra. Digvijaya means conquest of the sky or the directions.

In ancient times, kings traversed the length and breath of their kingdoms in ceremonial processions.

In the corporate world, the leader must travel through departments and ensure that he is seen and that his vision is known to all. Often leaders let their team do the talking. This creates an impression that the king is a puppet or has no mind of his own. A true leader needs to perform Digvijaya yatra to assert his authority and to tell the world where he plans to lead them and how.

Finally, there is the Vajapeya, a yagna of regeneration. This was done by kings from time to time to reinforce their authority. Make a head roll to tell the world who the boss is, for people's memories are often short.

11

Kurukshetra counsel

Of the eighteen days of the Kurukshetra battle described in the Mahabharata, nine days were indecisive. The Kauravas, with eleven armies, outnumbered the seven armies of the Pandavas. For the Pandavas, it was critical that Bhisma, the old but very able commander of the Kaurava forces, be killed.

So Krishna decided to make Shikhandi ride on his chariot alongside Arjuna. Shikhandi was born with the body of a woman which later transformed into the body of a man. Bhisma believed that a creature such as this was a woman and so refused to raise his bow against her. The Kauravas protested her entry into the battlefield but the Pandavas saw Shikhandi as a man. Arjuna had no qualms about using him/ her as a human shield, raising his bow at the invincible Bhisma and pinning him to the ground with hundreds of arrows.

Bhisma can be seen as a man who is paralysed by his own

interpretation of a situation. But any situation can be seen in many different ways. Through alternative interpretation, it is possible to challenge anyone. Defeat is inevitable if one is unable to accommodate an alternative point of view. Had Bhisma accepted that Shikhandi was a man, there was no way he could have been defeated.

Drona, the commander of the Kaurava army after Bhisma, was a ruthless killer, who broke the Pandava morale by killing Arjuna's son Abhimanyu and even making his soldiers fight at night, against the rule of war. To defeat him, Krishna spread the rumour that Ashwatthama was dead. Ashwatthama happened to be the name of Drona's son and Drona was extremely attached to him.

Ashwatthama was the reason for Drona's life. On hearing this rumour, his heart sank. Was his son dead? Yes, said all the Pandava warriors surrounding him. Yes, said Krishna. Drona turned to Yudhishthira, the most upright Pandava. Yudhishthira knew that the Ashwatthama being referred to was an elephant. Still he told Drona—either a man or an elephant, Ashwatthama is surely dead.

In the din of the battle, looking at the petrified face of Yudhishthira, Drona was convinced that his son was dead and that Yudhishthira gave him the strange answer to break the terrible news gently. He lowered his weapons. Taking advantage of this, the leader of the Pandava army raised his sword and beheaded Drona.

Drona can be seen as a man who is extremely attached to something personal. To break such a man down, that which he is attached to must be destroyed. Or at least he must be given the impression that it is destroyed. His obsession will cloud his judgement; he will not bother to delve deeper and check the facts. Many leaders have strong likes and dislikes and this can be used by corporate spin doctors and gossip-mongers to destroy relationships. Leaders have to be wary of this. They must check facts especially if the news relates to those who matter most to them. Otherwise, like Drona, they will end up beheaded.

Shalya, who became commander of the Kaurava army on the last day, had, according to the Indonesian Mahabharata, a demon that came out of his ears every time he was attacked. This demon became stronger if the attack against Shalya became more intense. To defeat Shalya, Krishna suggested that Yudhishthira fight him, not with rage but with love. So Yudhishthira walked towards Shalya with great affection. The demon in Shalya became so weak that it could not even come out of Shalya's ears. Yudhishthira came close to Shalya, with no malice in his heart, raised his spear and impaled the last leader of the Kauravas.

A powerful lesson here. There are people who become strong in confrontations. Such people must never be confronted. Their point must not be validated through arguments. The best way to invalidate them is to simply agree with them. This unnerves them. They come prepared to face all arguments and, in the absence of any, feel disempowered. Confused, they become vulnerable. People around them, seeing there is no one arguing their point, will withdraw. Thus through agreement can a point of view be destroyed.

Barbareek is a little-known character whose tale is told in many folk Mahabharatas. He was the son of Bhima by a snake princess and was stronger than all five Pandavas put together. Not wanting him to join the Kauravas, Krishna asked him for a boon. Barbareek was too nice a man to say no. So Krishna said, 'Give me your head.' Barbareek immediately severed his neck and offered his head to Krishna with one request that he be allowed to see this great battle from a vantage point. Krishna therefore placed his head on a hill that overlooked '. At the end of the war, the Pandavas asked him who the greatest warrior in the battlefield was. Barbareek replied, 'I saw no great warrior on the battlefield. All I saw was Krishna's discuss whirring around cutting the heads of warriors and their blood washing the hair of Draupadi, who had long ago been publicly disrobed by the very same warriors.'

It is a good idea, in the middle of corporate political wrangling, to step back and see who is provoking the fight and stoking the flames. Often the two parties involved fail to realize that out there is another man making them fight for his very own agenda. So ask yourself—are you fighting your own battle in Kurukshetra or are you a pawn in someone else's much bigger game?

12

The Vishwaroopa complex

 Vishwaroopa was the form taken by Krishna in the battlefield of Kurukshetra when Arjuna asked him to reveal his true form. In this form, Krishna no longer looks familiar. He is neither cowherd nor charioteer. He is a magnificent being with countless legs and countless arms and countless heads, breathing fire, containing within himself all the things that exist—all the worlds, all the animate beings and inanimate objects. It is an awe-inspiring sight containing everything that Arjuna imagined and also everything that was beyond Arjuna's imagination.

Increasingly, people, especially those who have been touched by success, are trying to become Vishwaroopas—expanding and trying to become everything and everyone simultaneously. Product manufactures are becoming service providers. Manufacturers are becoming marketers. Industrialists are becoming retailers. Hoteliers are becoming teachers. Because organizations are developing countless arms and countless legs to 'satisfy every element of the value chain'.

Dr Ramesh is a case in point. He was a celebrated cardiac surgeon. He performed six heart surgeries a day. He charged rupees one lakh as his consulting and operating fee per procedure. That did not include the cost of the operating theatre or the cost of hospital services or the drugs. That did not include the commission he got from everything that was spent on the operation. He was undoubtedly a very talented surgeon with a 99 per cent success rate. Every patient brought in more patients. Everyone loved him. Everyone wanted to felicitate him. He was a much sought-after teacher and mentor. Every day he looked at the adoring eyes of the patients, their families, his students, his staff, the nurses, the paramedics and the hospital administrators. Soon he concluded that he was perfect, he could do no wrong. Why then was he satisfied working in a hospital? Why could he not build a hospital of his own? He had hardly expressed this thought than the sponsors arrived and the land was made available. Before long his day was filled not with patients but with builders and sponsors and architects and administrators. He was talking business plans, growth, and profit and loss. He realized that his opinions not only mattered, they were good. Soon he was involved full-time in the building of his hospital. Then he realized, why be satisfied with one hospital? Why not build a chain in every city of his state, maybe the country? And then he thought, 'What good is a medical hospital without a medical college? And why not a nursing college?' And then he thought, 'Why buy branded pharmaceutical products which are so expensive—why not buy a generic company that could make all the products needed in the hospital at a fraction of the price?' In a short time, he had plans on pharmaceutical business, on a medical device business, on medical education, on hospitals, and even on retail pharmacies. He did not feel the need to perform heart surgeries anymore. Students who trained under him were as brilliant and could replicate what he did. Now he was focusing on his grand vision—providing heart surgeries to all who needed them. But slowly he was inching towards an ever grander vision, beyond heart surgeries—providing all health facilities to all those who needed them. In fact he was already in talks with people who believed his hospitals should provide treatment even to patients with joint problems and kidney problems and respiratory problems. Because the opportunities were huge, and his brand value that attracts funding was great.

This meteoric transformation is awe-inspiring and commendable, but when Arjuna saw Krishna's true form, he was scared and confused. He begged Krishna, 'Please come back to your original form. Vishwaroopa dazzles me, but I want my friend back.' At once, Vishwaroopa became Krishna, complete with cherubic smile and mischievous eyes. This was not Rama with the bow or Parashurama with the axe. This was not Shiva smeared with ash. This was not Lakshmi bedecked with gold and lotus flowers or Kali with blood-smeared tongue. This was a unique form of God, dark with a peacock feather and yellow dhoti, satisfying Arjuna's particular needs.

In Hindu belief, when all gods and goddesses, each with their distinguishing symbols, are combined into one whole, they become formless—nirguna, without form and beyond form. This is a grand concept but rather intangible and unfathomable for the common mind. Even Vishwaroopa, a form that contains everything, is rarely worshipped. Certainly not as much as a Krishna or a Rama. Each Hindu deity has his or her own identity manifesting as unique symbols. And while everyone knows that each one of them is part of the whole, attention and devotion are given to the part and not the whole.

In the Upanishads, which celebrate the oneness and unity of all things, there is also great value given in identifying what distinguishes one from the rest. Who are we? 'Iti-iti', this too and that too. Or 'neti-neti', not this and not that. This is one aspect we forget when success sparks within us the desire to expand and become Vishwaroopa. We start believing we are capable of everything. And as we plunge into our journey, we lose our individual characteristic symbols—the core of our being. As Krishna starts becoming Vishwaroopa, he becomes increasingly disconnected from Arjuna.

While Dr Ramesh's transformation from a surgeon to an entrepreneur is indeed awe-inspiring, he needs to step back and ask himself what he desires to become eventually. Does he want to totally stop connecting individually with patients? Does he want to focus exclusively on statistics and balance sheets? More importantly, he needs to ask himself: What does he desire *not* to become? Where does he draw the line?

Krishna must never be confused with Rama. Lakshmi must never be confused with Kali. Krishna is as much about what he *is* and what he *is not*. This clarification will ensure that Dr Ramesh, in his quest to become everything and everyone, does not end up becoming nothing and no one.

13

Waiting to exile

 In the Ramayana, Rama is asked to string a bow—a feat that will win him the hand of Sita in marriage. Rama, however, bends the bow with such force that it breaks. Since no one until then had even been able to pick up this bow, Sita's father is so impressed with Rama that he is more than happy to accept him as his son-in-law.

One cannot help but wonder: Why did Rama, known for his obedience, break a bow that was supposed to be strung? The bow is an ancient symbol of kingship. It represents poise and balance, useful only if the string is neither too loose nor too tight. That Rama, the ideal king, breaks a bow in his youth is surely an act of some significance. No ordinary bow this, but the bow of Shiva, the great ascetic.

Rama's father feels that with a wife by his side, Rama is now old enough to be king and so declares his decision to retire.

Unfortunately, the planned coronation does not take place. Palace intrigues force Rama to go into forest exile instead. Is there a correlation between the breaking of the bow and the denial of his kingship? The epic does not say so explicitly. Nor has any scholar commented on it. But the question is an interesting one. After all, everything in Hindu narratives is symbolic and there is surely a meaning here that is waiting to be decoded.

Rama's breaking of Shiva's bow probably suggests an act of passion and attachment, for Shiva is the god of renunciation and detachment. Is that why he is considered unfit to be king? Is that why he must go into the forest for fourteen years, and return only when he has cultivated adequate detachment? Observe the almost inhuman lack of passion displayed by Rama, fourteen years later, when he finally kills Ravana and rescues his wife Sita. He tells her that he killed Ravana not to rescue her but to uphold dharma and clear his family's honour. It is almost as if showing feelings for one's spouse is unacceptable for one who seeks to be king. He had shown his passion once, when he broke the bow. He shall not do so again.

The ancient seers demanded such detachment from kings. Kingship had to be more important than family. That is why Rama is put on the highest pedestal. One may not quite agree with this philosophy today, but it is clear that the epic considers the years in the wilderness not as a tragedy but as a period to mature until one is ready to truly wear the crown.

This theme of 'growing up' in the wilderness is repeated in the Mahabharata. Krishna helps the Pandavas establish the kingdom of Indraprastha. But the five brothers foolishly gamble away their kingdom in Krishna's absence, a crime for which they have to suffer thirteen years of exile including one year incognito. When Yudhishthira moans his fate, the sages tell him the story of Rama who suffered fourteen years of exile, one year more than them, and that too for no fault of his. They tell the Pandavas to stop whining and use the period in the forest to learn. And they learn: Arjuna learns humility when he is defeated by a common hunter (Shiva in disguise) in battle; Bhima learns humility when he is unable to lift the tail of an old monkey (Hanuman in disguise); and all the brothers learn humility when they are forced to live as servants in the final year of exile. Only then does Krishna lead them to a triumphant battle against their enemies.

Most leaders who have done anything worthwhile in the corporate world have had their own forest exile. Talk to any CEO, or successful entrepreneur, and they will tell of their years in the corporate wilderness, when no one respected them, when they were pushed down and not given what was due to them, when they were kept away from power by lesser men, men who feared them. They will tell you of a time when they were treated as wannabes, or worse, as has-beens. Unfortunately, many leaders do not take such periods of corporate exile positively. It makes them bitter and more insecure. Rather than become phoenixes, brilliant mythical birds who rise from their own ashes, they turn into banyan trees, giving comfort to all but not letting even a blade of grass grow in their shade.

It has been observed that one leader of a medium-sized company loves to give every member of his team the impression that they are powerful. But the truth is that he is the sole decision maker. He has not created a talent pool, a second line of command. Ask him why, and he will refuse to acknowledge this very evident truth. Perhaps he is not even aware of it. There was a time when he headed a marketing division of another company with high growth prospects. But when a new CEO took over the company, he fell out of favour and was shunted out, given a high-sounding lowly post in a faraway country for three years. Those three years in the corporate wilderness shattered him. He became bitter and aggressive, determined to fight back and emerge a winner. In rage he left the organization and joined a new one and now, after years of struggle, is back—heading a bigger organization, in a far higher position than all those who shunted him out. He is enjoying every moment of his triumphant return. He has shown them!

But the event has taken its toll—he is not the generous man he once was. He looks upon everyone as a potential threat, a future back-stabber. His actions and influence on the organization display a pessimism that has seeped into his being. He lacks the hope that he should have discovered in the days of his struggle. Once a victim, he has now become a victimizer, perpetuating the vicious cycle of bitter exiles and vengeful returns.

The scriptures frown upon such myopic leadership. It reeks of lack of character and a lack of faith in the bigger picture. Both epics view the forest exile as opportunities to discover inner strengths and return as greater men. Had Rama not gone to the forest, he would not have triumphed over Ravana, and had the Pandavas not suffered the exile, they would not have had the moral high ground over their enemies. Ultimately, after a long period of glorious rule, both Rama and the Pandavas voluntarily give up their crown, passing it on to the next generation of worthy rulers, illustrating to all that ultimately every leader has to move on.

14

The laws of the jungle

One day, states the *Bhagavata Purana,* the earth-goddess took the form of a cow and went to Vishnu with tears in her eyes, complaining how the kings of the earth were exploiting her. Her udders were sore, squeezed by human greed. Vishnu promised to set things right and so descended on earth as Krishna.

In the Mahabharata, however, Krishna advises the Pandavas to set a forest aflame. This forest, Khandavaprastha, is the share of property given to the Pandavas by their uncle Dhritarashtra when they demand their inheritance. As the trees burn, the animals and birds of the forest try to escape. Krishna instructs Arjuna to circle the forest on his chariot and shoot down every escaping bird and beast. Hundreds of animals are thus massacred, the rest roasted alive. The serpents beg the rain-god, Indra, to come to their rescue. But

71

again, on Krishna's advice, Arjuna uses his arrows to create a canopy over the forest, preventing the water from dousing the flames. None are spared except an asura called Maya on condition that he build for the Pandavas on the gutted land a magnificent city called Indraprastha, which goes on to become the greatest city in the world.

On one hand, Vishnu promises to protect the earth from humans; on the other hand, Krishna himself indulges in an activity that damages the earth. What is happening?

These two stories draw attention to the nature of human civilization and one unspoken aspect of leadership and organization: the power of authority.

Nature is intrinsically wild—wanting to go its own way. Nature's order is created through the game of survival. Every creature is on its own. Through strength or cunning, every plant and animal can make their own space. Those who are unable to withstand the opposition or exploit the opportunity wither away and die. Nature is thus generous on one hand, giving total freedom and all possibilities to the mighty, and indifferent on the other, offering no help to the meek.

The human mind rejects this state of being. Humans have the power to reorganize the rules of nature so that life becomes more predictable and secure, and one can look beyond survival. When the Pandavas declare their intention to become king, they are essentially saying they are unwilling to accept the natural state of things. They wish to domesticate nature so that all creatures align to a set of rules—their rules. This means destruction of all other rules and laws.

Nature has two parts: the mind (internal nature) and the forest (external nature). Both need to be tamed. The king ensures that the mind of his people is disciplined and aligned to his way of thinking and performing through logic, reward, punishment and constant coaching. The trees and creepers of the forest are destroyed to make way for fields and orchards where only the seed chosen by the king is planted. All other plants that attempt to grow on the king's land are declared weeds—to be pulled out and cast away. A culture is born where it is clear what is acceptable and what is not, what is right and what is wrong. The benchmark of such judgements is laid down by the king.

From one point of view, a king and leader is doing a good thing—creating resources and opportunities for his people by laying down the law. But on the other hand he is curbing freedom or at least controlling it. A king has no choice but to tread this delicate line.

In the Mahabharata, during their exile in the forest, the sages tell the Pandavas the story of Ushinara, king of Shibi. One day, a dove came to the king and begged him to grant it protection. When the king promised to protect it, a hawk, who was pursuing the dove, asked, 'What will I eat then?' The king told the hawk to eat any other dove but this one. The hawk argued that that was unfair: Why should other doves be sacrificed so that the king could keep his promise to his dove? The king then requested the hawk to eat any other bird or beast. The hawk argued that that too was unfair: Why should other birds and beasts be sacrificed so that the king could keep his promise to his dove? 'Then eat me,' said the king, offering pieces of his flesh. These were placed on a balancing scale so that the hawk got flesh equal in measure to the dove's weight. To the astonishment of the king, the dove was so heavy that he had to give up almost all the flesh of his body.

Typically, the story is narrated to extol the virtues of the king's kindness and sacrifice. But there is an underlying wisdom in this story. In nature, hawks eat doves. By introducing the human virtue of kindness into the natural law, the king could not make both the hawk and the dove happy. Either the dove had to die or the hawk had to go starving. Since neither was acceptable, the king had to die. If kings have to thrive, someone will benefit and someone will suffer. The king's authority cannot make everyone happy—either the animals will thrive or the city will be built. This tough lesson is taught to the Pandavas when the forest of Khandavaprastha is burnt to make way for Indraprastha.

That being said, the scriptures repeatedly tell the story of Vena, a king who so excessively plundered the earth that the sages were forced to kill him using a blade of grass that they transformed into a potent missile using magical mantras. Then the king's corpse was churned. All negative aspects of the king were cast away and a purer, nobler king, Prithu, was created. The gods declared Prithu the new king by giving him a bow. The earth, still reeling under the impact of Vena's reign, refused to let the seeds sprout and the plants flower and bear fruit. Taking the form of a cow she ran away and Prithu chased her on his chariot, his new bow in hand. 'If you kill me, all life will end,' said the earth-cow. Prithu then lowered his bow and begged the earth to feed his subjects. He promised to be a king who treats the earth as a cowherd treats a cow. He would love her, protect her and nurture her. In exchange she would provide milk and dung that would be the food and fuel of human civilization. She would be Go-mata, the cow mother, and he would be Go-pala, the cow keeper.

Thus Prithu realizes the bow was given to him by the gods not to hunt the earth down or to domesticate her and strip her of her wildness but to learn the importance of balance. A bow is useless if the string is too loose; it will break if the string is too tight. Likewise, a king has to balance his desire to control and domesticate nature with the wisdom to let nature be and thrive freely. A good king knows when to stop; how much of the forest should be burnt and how much should not. How much alignment he should seek and how much freedom he must give.

15

Common corporate culture beyond belief

Most people in the corporate world have been educated in the modern scientific education system. They have gone through school where they learnt language, mathematics, science, history, and geography. Then they went through college specializing either in science or arts or commerce. And yet, despite a relatively standardized education system, everyone is different.

Do these differences matter? Do we simply focus on their qualifications, knowledge and skills, and ignore the influence of culture? Different cultures look at the world differently. And this affects their attitude to life and work. Half the world, for example, believes there is life after death. The other half believes there is no life after death. One half of the world believes life is determined by fate. The other half believes life is determined by free will.

Who is right? Do such belief systems affect our day-to-day conduct at work? Will a person who subscribes to fatalism have the same drive as one who believes in free will? Who will have a greater sense of urgency—one who believes there is only one life with only one chance or one who believes this is just one of the many lives one can live? Differences in cultures manifest in the stories they tell.

The earliest Greek epics, the Iliad and the Odyssey, are tales of heroes—Achilles in the one and Odysseus in the other. Both face calamities thrust upon them by angry gods. In the Iliad, it is Apollo who shoots arrows of disease at the Greek army, prompting a series of events that so infuriates the passionate Achilles that he withdraws from the battlefield. In the Odyssey, it is the sea-god Poseidon whose storms delay the homecoming of Odysseus by ten years.

In both cases, the men triumph against the odds through sheer grit and determination. The gods are unable to hold them back. Both epics glorify the refusal of man to submit to the boundaries imposed by God. Greatness lies in transgression. These Greek epics inspired what is today recognized as the Western celebration of the individual spirit.

But the West is influenced by another great epic—the Bible. Biblical stories, which evolved in the Near East and the Middle East, belong to a heritage that is common to Jews, Christians and Muslims. In these tales there are no gods. There was one almighty God (spelt in singular and capitalized).

Unlike the gods, this God is not threatened by man; he loves man. He casts man out of Heaven when man transgresses his laws. Return is possible to the primal bliss only by submitting to the wisdom of the divine. Unlike the Greek way, glory lies not in transgression but in obedience. Now compare these with the earliest Hindu epics—the Ramayana and the Mahabharata.

These are not tales of individual heroes. These are family dramas, tales of householders, men whose glory came not from lonely adventures far away from home but through engagement with relatives—brothers, sisters, fathers, mothers, husbands, wives, sons and daughters.

These epics have gods (devas) and God (Bhagavan). There are even goddesses (Sachi and Ganga) and Goddesses (Lakshmi, Durga). Here the hero is God. But he is also mortal. The divine exists here not to create problems or laws for man but to teach man how to cope with the problems of life.

The approach is different in both epics. In the Ramayana, the protagonist, Rama, sacrifices everything to uphold the law while in the Mahabharata, the protagonist, Krishna, keeps breaking the law. Both upholding and breaking the law are done in the pursuit of dharma. This word means stability, order, righteousness.

Variation in approach is attributed to the fact that the two belong to different periods in time—Rama belongs to Treta Yuga while Krishna belongs to Dvapara Yuga. Everything is contextual. But dharma does not bring permanence. Eventually the world will collapse. After death will come rebirth; another world with another Treta Yuga, and another Dvapara Yuga with another Rama and another Krishna.

Both the Greek and Biblical ways assume there is only

one life and only one way to live life: individual achievement according to the Greeks, and collective surrender for the Jews, Christians and Muslims. In the Hindu way, as in the Buddhist and Jain way, there are many lives. Everything is cyclical and repetitive. The only way to make sense of this merry-go-round is to step back and reflect on life.

Do these cultures matter in the corporate world? They do, because all of us are churned out of these cultures. Over time, these cultures have mingled and merged with each other. Hence a little bit of all cultures lies within us.

When you think logical and behave individualistically, know that the seed was planted into human thought by the Greeks. When you reject hierarchy, embrace community and surrender to a higher reality before whom all are equal, recognize its roots in the Biblical tradition. When you think contextual, thank the Hindus. The Chinese gave the world the value of harmony (Tao) and the need to organize flux through ritual and discipline (Confucius).

Some of these traits are more dominant than others. This becomes obvious when, despite intense attempts to create a common corporate culture, one notices the attitudinal and behavioural differences amongst employees of the same MNC belonging to different countries. A leader may be an MBA from Harvard—but it will always matter whether he is White or Black, Christian or Muslim, Indian or Nepalese, gay or straight, Bengali or Tamilian, Brahmin or Dalit. The global village may never ever have a single attitude towards work and life. And this is not necessarily a bad thing.

Leader: 50 Insights from Mythology

16

Eyes of a leader

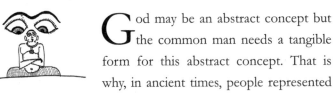God may be an abstract concept but the common man needs a tangible form for this abstract concept. That is why, in ancient times, people represented their deities as rocks. That is why, when we travel across India, we find in shrines of local gods and goddesses, no elaborate imagery, just a rock smeared with turmeric or saffron or vermillion. But such imagery is too impersonal. To make it personal, in many shrines, one thing is done—the rock is given eyes, large petal-shaped eyes, usually of metal. They stare at the devotees constantly from the moment the door of the shrine is opened to the time the shrine is shut. In temples, the ritual that transforms an ordinary statue into a deity is called the 'eye-bestowing ceremony'. Once the eye is given, or opened, the deity is established and alive. The murti becomes swarup, the living image of the divine. What is so

special about the eye? What does the eye do? And why is the eye equated with life?

With the appearance of the eye, the stone becomes sentient—it can sense, it can see, it can respond to the world in front of it. The eye-bestowing ritual tells us something very powerful about humans, about the devotees who establish the deity. We want to be seen. We want our gods to observe us, know us and understand us. Without eyes, how can they know our pain, our aspirations and our issues? We constantly ask God to open his eyes, see our suffering and even shed tears for us, empathizing with our situation. A leader is supposed to be like that village god or goddess: he or she must have eyes that observe the team and understand them for who they really are.

The Mahabharata tells the story of a kingdom where the royal couple has no eyes. The king, Dhritarashtra, is blind, and his queen, Gandhari, is blindfolded. The result: children who feel unobserved. The father cannot see; the mother chooses not to see. The children grow up with a warped value system. Since no one is seeing them, they feel they can get away with anything. As a result the law of the jungle reigns supreme in the kingdom of Dhritarashtra. A woman is publicly disrobed and lands are grabbed by force.

A leader must see his people. He must recognize them for who they are, rather than what he wants them to be. More often than not, leaders don't have eyes—or rather they see only themselves. Their eyes are only for their vision of the world. They do not realize there are others around them with other visions of life. This lack of eyes strips them of all empathy. Everything is measured and valued against their own vision. Those who align with their vision are good; those who fail to do so are bad. Intellectual leaders with an intellectual outlook of things, therefore, look down upon people who are not intellectual. Emotional leaders keep advising non-emotional team members to transform for their betterment. Task-oriented leaders do not value people-oriented team members and vice versa. In other words, they see nothing but themselves and constantly seek themselves in others. They notice no one else.

Aziz knows what it feels to have a blind boss. Due to unfortunate circumstances, Aziz could not study beyond the twelfth standard. A contact brought him to a garment manufacturing unit where the proprietor, Jaichand-saab, decided to make him the telephone operator because he spoke English. Aziz had no choice but to accept the position. But in a matter of a few weeks, he knew everything about the garment business simply by answering the queries on the telephone: he knew where sourcing was done, where the finances came from, what the customers were looking for, what the issues were in the garment manufacturing business, who were the competitors. Every time he tried to talk to Jaichand-saab of a way to improve the business, Jaichand-saab dismissed him because for Jaichand-saab, Aziz remained a 'twelfth standard pass, English-speaking, telephone operator'. Blinded by Aziz's resumé, he refused to see Aziz—the living, breathing, thinking, feeling Aziz. He did not see, or even try to see, the person before him.

One day, Jaichand-saab's son, Krishnachand, came to the office to help his father. Krishnachand noticed that Aziz was different from the other employees. He could answer all queries. So he knew everything, but could he imagine? The owner's son took Aziz out for lunch. It was an unforgettable lunch: he discovered how brilliant Aziz was—he had imagination and creativity, an ability to diagnose problems and find innovative solutions. He was all excited to tell his father about the discovery. But when he returned to the office, he had to face an angry father. Jaichand-saab shouted at his son, 'Don't get too familiar with the workers!' Out of respect, knowing his father, Krishnachand kept quiet. It struck him how blind his father was. He did not blame his father; after all, when was the last time his father actually saw him? One day, thought Krishnachand, he would take over the business. That day, he would make Aziz his right-hand man, whatever his qualifications.

The ability to recognize and nurture talent is often missing in people who are assumed to be leaders by their respective organizations. Some leaders recognize talent but do not know what to do with it. Others, envious of talent, reject or ignore them deliberately. The character Karna in the Mahabharata is a case in point. Like Aziz, who is dismissed as 'twelfth standard pass, English-speaking, telephone operator', Karna was always seen as a charioteer's son and never as a great archer by the Pandavas. Only Duryodhana saw Karna's talent but used him, unfortunately, for his villainous goals. This is what happens to talented people who are rejected by the mainstream—they end up in the wrong hands. And in rage and frustration, they end up doing the undesirable.

In the Upanishads, it is said that it is an observer who creates an observation. It is our attention that creates the world around us. Thus it is the eyes of the village deity that creates the village around him. Likewise, it is the eyes of the leader that creates an organization around him. Dhritarashtra's lack of sight and his wife's refusal to see created the Kauravas. It is not so much about sight as it is about attention—how much attention we put in people around us. We want the gods to see us and pay attention to us. Do we see people around us and pay attention to them? Do we see what they see? Do we try and align our vision to theirs or do we simply impose our vision on to them? It is time for leaders to open their eyes to these questions.

17

Strategic intent of Ravana

 With ten heads, twenty arms, a flying chariot, and a city of gold, Ravana is one of the most flamboyant villains in Hindu mythology. He abducted Sita, the wife of Rama, and was struck down for that. Ravana is the demon king of the Ramayana, the lord of the rakshasas, whose effigy must be burnt each year in the autumn festival commemorating the victory of Rama.

Yet, there is much about him to be admired—he was a poet who composed the Rudra Stotra in praise of Shiva, the ascetic god; he was a musician who used one of his heads and one of his arms to design a lute called Rudra Veena, in honour of Shiva. When Hanuman entered Lanka, in search of Sita, he found the demon lord lying in bed surrounded by a bevy of beauties, women who, drawn by Ravana's sexual prowess, had willingly abandoned their husbands. Rishi Agastya informed

Rama that Ravana was only half-demon: his father, Vaishrava, was a Brahmin whose father was Pulastya, one of the seven mind-born primal sons of Brahma himself. So after killing Ravana, before returning to Ayodhya, Rama went to the Himalayas to perform penance and purify himself of the sin of Brahma-hatya or the killing of a Brahmin.

Rama, by comparison, seems boring—an upholder of rules who never does anything spontaneous or dramatic. He always does the right thing, whether he likes it or not, and does not seem like much fun. It is natural therefore to be a fan of Ravana, to be seduced by his power, to be enchanted by his glamour, and to find arguments that justify his actions.

In the corporate world, flamboyant CEOs do get a lot of attention, especially if they also happen to be successful CEOs, with their very own city of gold built on rising stock markets. One is dazzled by the cars they drive, the lives they lead, their swagger, their confidence, their individual aura that makes them giants amongst their peers, powerful men like Trilochanji who command authority and demand allegiance. Trilochanji's team admires the way he can pick up the phone and get things done. He has the money to buy anybody who stands in his way. And the political clout to get all the clearances. He has, in a short while, managed to grow his business at a rate that his predecessors could only imagine. Trilochanji's organization is in awe of him. And everyone fears him.

By contrast, Asutoshji, Trilochanji's cousin, is a very mild man. His business has grown rapidly too, but no one knows about it, because he does not push his public relations department too much. Why? 'Because press coverage has no impact on my business.' He meticulously gathers data, plans his strategies with his team, empowers his directors to implement them thoroughly, keeps a hawk's eye on deviations, and ensures the numbers are met. Few would notice him in the office. He dresses like others do, uses the same toilet as his employees, loves spending his Sundays only with family, and is happiest when he can give his employees a good bonus and his shareholders a good dividend. Not the best results in the market, but much better than last year. The point, he says, is not show-spikes of brilliance but a steady sustainable growth. His speeches are boring, too accurate, and lack the glamour of Trilochanji's. And when in crisis, Asutoshji will not pick up the phone to call a politician, nor will he look for people he can buy out; he will meticulously plan his action to solve the problem without looking for short cuts. 'Because,' he says, 'short cuts always have long-term repercussions and I will not risk it while I am the custodian of my company's future.'

It is simplistic to call Trilochanji a Ravana and Asutoshji a Rama simply because the former is flamboyant and commanding while the latter is boring and task-oriented. What makes Ravana villain of the Ramayana is not his heads, or arms, or flying chariot or city of gold. It is his strategic intent.

What does Ravana stand for? He never built the city of gold—he drove out his brother, Kubera, and took over the kingdom of Lanka. He went around the world killing sages and raping women. Why? To establish his dominion and to generate fear. Why did he abduct Sita? Avenging his sister's mutilation was but an excuse; it was the desire to conquer the heart of a faithful wife. And during the war, he let his sons and his brothers die before entering the battlefield himself. His desire for victory over Sita and Rama mattered more than the lives of his people.

Ravana lives only for himself. His pleasure matters the most. Ironically, he is a devotee of Shiva—the ascetic, the god who demonstrates his disdain for all things material and sensuous by smearing his body with ash and living in crematoriums and atop a desolate icy hill. Ravana may sing praises of Shiva and bow to him, but despite having ten heads is unable to internalize the wisdom of Shiva. Maybe he does understand Shiva's ascetic philosophy intellectually, enabling him to compose potent hymns, but he is unable to follow Shiva's way in spirit. For all his prayers and poems, he remains attached to power and pleasure and wealth—all things material, and all things transitory. He is no nihilist; he is simply a weak man, a talker, not a doer.

In Hindu mythology, a leader is not one who rules a city of gold or travels on a flying chariot. He is one who lives to make a positive impact on the lives of others. Leadership is not about self-aggrandizement. It is about creating a society where people can live a full life. Rama is hero and God, not because he is a boring obedient son, but because by being an obedient son, he demonstrates his commitment to 'others'. He lives not for his pleasure, as Ravana does, but for the pleasure of those around him. And the journey is not easy—for one can never please everybody. Trilochanji's empire is a by-product of his desire to dominate and be feared while Asutoshji establishes businesses to satisfy his employees and consumers to the best of his ability. It is the difference in strategic intent that makes one Ravana and the other Rama.

18

Vikramaditya and Vetal

Vikramaditya, king of Ujjain, pulled down the ghost or Vetal who swung upside down from the branches of a tree that grew on the edge of a crematorium ground. 'If you can bring this creature to me,' a sorcerer had told the king, 'I can turn him into a mighty slave who will do all your bidding. But remember, while you are carrying Vetal, you must never speak. One word from your lips and he will fly back to his tree.' Vikramaditya swore, as he walked towards the tree, to keep his mouth shut. Vetal did not mind this, more than happy to fill the silence with an entertaining tale:

Once upon a time, a king was performing the funeral rites for his father. As he was about to drop the funeral offering in the river, as ritual demanded, three hands rose from the water to receive it. The first hand belonged to a weaver, to whom the king's mother had been forcibly given in marriage. The second hand was of a priest who loved the king's mother and had made her pregnant. The third was of a warrior who had found the king abandoned on the riverbank and had adopted him and raised him as his own. 'Now tell me, Vikramaditya,' said Vetal, 'on which hand should the king place the funeral offering? On the hand of his mother's husband, on the hand of his biological father or the hand of his foster-father? On the hand of the weaver, the priest or the warrior? If you know the answer, speak and complete the story, or the sin of keeping a story incomplete will cause your head to burst into a thousand pieces.'

Can there an objective answer to this question? In modern times, a child's father is determined by a biological paternity test but the results can be dismissed by the legal adoption process. In the Mahabharata, however, marriage was most important in determining paternity. That is why Pandu is identified as the father of the five Pandavas even though he did not make either of his wives pregnant.

The story of Vikramaditya and Vetal draws attention to the fact that in the world not every question has an obvious objective answer. Many questions demand subjective answers—a call. And the man who makes the call is the leader. He is Vikramaditya.

Ruchika is a Vikramaditya. She runs a boutique chain that sells high fashion. She has an immediate task at hand: to select a model who will appear in hoardings and print ads over the next six months. The budget is huge and before her is a complete SWOT analysis including the cost of the top models, the market perception of each of the models, their current brand equity, and future trends. Ruchika knows that in selecting the model, she will effectively be selecting the brand image of her stores. Does she want to continue with the image that exists? Does she want to change it? What will be the consequences of this creative decision? Will it change the quality of footfalls to the shops? Will she get the teenage crowd or the family crowd? Her choice of model will influence many things. She turns to her finance team who give her the financial implications of her business decision—the optimistic and the pessimistic picture. There is no consensus in her design or sales team. For some the cool new model matters, others prefer the classical, and then there are those who want to be radical.

For all that talk about taking a decision as a team, Ruchika knows that ultimately she will have to take a call. If only she had the luxury of not saying anything. But then Ruchika realizes, she has not been made the head of the organization to keep quiet. She is the leader. She must use her intelligence and her intuition and arrive at a decision, howsoever subjective it may be, a decision that will affect the future of her company, her employees, her customers, her balance sheet and ultimately her own career. She must think, she must decide, she must speak. And her decision will not please everyone. They will oppose her, criticize her, pull her down when her decision does not yield the desired outcomes. She will have no one to blame, no one to hide behind. The buck stops with her. That is the price of kingship. That is the curse of Vikramaditya.

Vikramaditya always gives an answer but in different

versions of the tale, the answer is different. Sometimes, valuing social institutions as the key to social order, he chooses the legal husband, the weaver. Sometimes, giving due cognizance to caste hierarchy, he declares the priest as the father. And sometimes, valuing the role of emotions, he convinces himself and Vetal that the warrior who raised the king is the true father. There is no right answer. There is no wrong answer. Everything depends on Vikramaditya's values—what according to him is right, what according to him is wrong. Values determines the nature of Vikramaditya's judgements and hence the quality of his kingdom.

If Vikramaditya believes that his judgement is objective, then he is only deluding himself. All decisions are moulded by frameworks and contexts—all frameworks are constructed and all contexts are interpreted through the subjective lens. Data helps but to a point, not beyond. That is why we cannot have an organization without kings. Ujjain is a prosperous city because Vikramaditya takes the right calls, or rather he takes calls that he feels are right and which turn out to be beneficial eventually. That is why Vikramaditya is a great king. Every king can take a call—but only a great king can take calls that consistently yield the desired outcomes.

Right or wrong, Vikramaditya has to speak, and let Vetal go, and start the process all over again. The day Vikramaditya has no answer, the fantasy of the sorcerer who will turn Vetal into a super-slave will take over and the reality of the brilliant king and his fabulous decision-making abilities will come to an end.

Leader: 50 Insights from Mythology

19

Lever of charity

Of the five tenets of Islam, there is one that forces the believer to take cognizance of others around him. The first tenet is about the faith one must have—faith in one God and his final prophet, Muhammad. The second is about prayer—five times every day. The third is about annual fasting—in the month of Ramzan when the word of God was revealed through the archangel Gabriel. The fourth is about a journey that must take place once in a lifetime—to the holy city of Mecca. The fifth one is of charity—keeping aside a portion of one's earnings for the benefit of others.

The first four tenets can be practised without acknowledging the other—one can believe, pray, fast and travel solitarily if one is determined to do so. But one cannot be charitable without considering others. Unless there is someone who can and will receive the charity, one cannot be charitable. Thus through the tenet of charity the individual is forced to care for the community. He is forced to look beyond his own interests at the needs of others.

This tenet is significant in the context of when it was first preached and to whom. The Arabs in the seventh century AD, and that includes Muhammad himself before he became the prophet, were mostly traders. Through Arabia the wealth of India and China reached Europe, since the Persian Empire had blocked all overland trade routes to Rome. The Arabs benefited greatly from this embargo. It was a boom time in the deserts, long before oil was discovered, long before Europeans found the sea routes to Asia, long before Islam was revealed to man. Islam transformed these hard-nosed traders. It forced them to look inwards and align themselves with the divine. More importantly, through the tenet of charity, it forced them to look beyond transactions, beyond their top and bottom-lines, at the world around them.

Increasingly, companies are trying to become more socially responsible—they are trying to look beyond their wallets. Its most recent manifestation is corporate social responsibility (CSR). But these exercises seem more like exercises to 'look good' and are often at odds with the organizational desire to 'win at any cost in the marketplace'. At least, Jayant feels so.

Jayant works as an area manager in a company that sells computer peripherals. He spends all day pushing his team to reach the sales target. Why? 'So that we can all make our bonuses,' he says. Jayant drives his team up the wall. 'You are paid to sell, so sell. It's your job.' Jayant has reduced his profession to a transaction—transaction with his company (reach target and get bonus) and with his customers (sell well because it is why what you are paid to do.) He is a thorough professional. He works with his team, draws up plans with them, reviews the plans, and comes up with innovative ideas to help them overcome a sticky situation. He coaches them, counsels them, motivates them, does all that is needed to win. But he does this as part of his job. And the company is happy with him. The account book is perfectly balanced between him and the organization on one hand and him and the customer on the other.

Now his company has got on to the CSR bandwagon. He is being asked to give a day's salary or an equal amount of time to a set of NGOs that the organization wants to help. He heard the MD say that the company will give away in charity an amount equal to the amount collected from employees. Jayant does not like this emotional arm-twisting into being charitable! He knows that refusal to participate in the programme will not be appreciated by the organization. It may even affect his chances of promotion. He is irritated. He joined the company to make money—not to give it away even if it is in charity.

The attitude of charity cannot be created by an organizational directive. It needs to be kindled internally in each employee. Employees participate only because they are obliged to—not because they want to. The problem lies in trying to make charity not a by-product of business, an incidental glance at society at large. The solution lies in making charity an integral part of the business. To be truly charitable, one has to find a way where charity enables business growth, not the other way around.

In Islam economic inequality is the work of the Devil. God made all creatures equal and gave everyone equal access to the world's resources. The Devil disrupted this equilibrium. Trade can never be enough to combat the Devil. One needs charity. One needed to go beyond transactions, and consciously and voluntarily help the other. Thus, charity is very much an essential part of the process that makes one a good Muslim. Surrender to the divine is not possible without developing a charitable spirit. How can this be done in an organization? How can Jayant be charitable while doing sales? How can charity become a tool to reach the target?

Jayant has not realized that he is already doing it. He is just not aware of it. For most of us charity is about giving money. But as the adage goes—people don't live by bread alone. People can be charitable in many ways—with time, with attention, with simply honing the desire to care. Has Jayant paid attention to his team—has he noticed that one of his team members is not performing well because he is worried about his wife who is suffering from chronic depression? Has Jayant paid attention to his clients: has he noticed that his most important client is annoyed with a colleague but has no friend with whom he can share this? Can Jayant be charitable to make sure that his work timings do not encroach into the personal free time of his teammates (he loves working on Sunday, his team does not)? Can Jayant be charitable enough to help his boss do whatever it takes to get the next promotion? When Jayant does all this he builds emotional equity which lubricates all transactions and helps business grow. When Jayant does it as a habit, charity gets embedded into his life and into the organizational culture. Then the organization does not have to ask Jayant to participate in CSR. He will do so voluntarily. CSR stops being an antidote of corporate guilt; it becomes the core of profitable behaviour.

20

Proactive Garuda

One day, Narada asked Vishnu, with a bit of hesitation, 'Why do you insist that the image of Garuda be placed before you in your temples? Why not me? Am I not your greatest devotee?' Before Vishnu could reply a crash was heard outside the main gate of Vaikuntha. 'What was that?' asked Vishnu. Narada turned to look in the direction of the sound. Garuda, Vishnu's hawk and vehicle, who usually investigated such events, was nowhere to be seen. 'I have sent Garuda on an errand. Can you find out what happened, Narada?' asked Vishnu. Eager to please Vishnu, Narada ran out to investigate. 'A milkmaid tripped and fell,' he said when he returned.

'What was her name?' asked Vishnu. Narada ran out, spoke to the maid and returned with the answer. 'Sharada,' he said. 'Where was she going?' asked Vishnu. Narada ran out once again, spoke to the maid and returned with the answer. 'She was on her way to the market.' 'What caused her to trip?' asked Vishnu. 'Why did you not ask this question the last time I went?' said Narada irritably. He then ran out, spoke to the maid once again. 'She was startled by a serpent that crossed her path,' he said on his return. 'Is the pot she was carrying broken?' asked Vishnu. 'I don't know,' snapped Narada. 'Find out,' said Vishnu. 'Why?' asked Narada. 'Find out, Narada. Maybe I would like to buy some milk,' said Vishnu. With great reluctance, Narada stepped out of Vaikuntha and met the milkmaid. He returned looking rather pleased, 'She broke one pot. But there is another one intact. And she is willing to sell the milk but at double price.'

'So how much should I pay her?' asked Vishnu. 'Oh, I forgot to ask. I am so sorry,' said Narada, running out once again. 'Do not bother. Let me send someone else,' said Vishnu.

Just then, Garuda flew in. He had no idea of what had transpired between Vishnu and Narada. Vishnu told Garuda, 'I heard a crashing sound outside the main gate. Can you find out what happened?' As Garuda left, Vishnu winked at Narada and whispered, 'Let us see how he fares.'

Garuda returned. 'It is a milkmaid called Sharada. She was on her way to the market. On the way, a snake crossed her path. Startled, she fell back and broke one of the two pots of milk she was carrying. Now she wonders how she will make enough money to pay for the broken pot and the spilt milk. I suggested she sell the milk to you. After all, you are married to Lakshmi, the goddess of wealth.'

'And the price of the milk?' asked Vishnu. Immediately

came Garuda's reply, 'Four copper coins. One actually, but I think she hopes to make a handsome profit when dealing with God.' Vishnu started to laugh. His eye caught Narada's and Narada understood at that instant why Garuda's statue and not his is always placed before the image of Vishnu in Vishnu temples.

Narada had behaved like a reactive subordinate. Very obedient, doing what the master told him to, leaving all the thinking to the master. Garuda behaved like a proactive subordinate, anticipating all his master's moves and preparing for it. That 'ability to anticipate' made Garuda more efficient and effective and hence more valuable in the eyes of Vishnu.

Kapur, senior vice-president of operations at a telecom firm has a simple method to distinguish the Garuda from the Narada in his team. During all his meetings, he assigns tasks to all team members. And he observes who comes to him with an update without his asking and who provides updates only when asked. He likes those people who approach him and give him feedback on projects proactively. They do not wait for a crisis. They don't wait for meetings. They don't wait to be asked.

Some of the best secretaries in the world are Garudas—they know what their boss wants even before the boss asks for it. They know that when they say, 'Book me a ticket to Jaipur' they are expected to make the hotel bookings and the car pickups, update the Blackberry with the appointments and reminders and alarms. They know what bills need to be processed at the first of the month, on the first Monday of every month, on the last day of every month. They know when the weekend parties have to be organized, when the stress level shoots up, when the bosses are more relaxed. They are sensitive to the rhythms of the boss, the rituals they follow. And all this comes from the 'ability to anticipate'.

Of course, insecure bosses can get annoyed, even threatened, by subordinates with the 'ability to anticipate'. They feel that if he knows my every move, he may one day overshadow me. This is what happened to Jiten who went out of his way to update his boss on everything he did, not waiting for his boss to ask him for updates. He knew the answers to every question asked by his boss. He seemed prepared for any argument or objection made by the boss. The boss said to himself, 'This man does everything so brilliantly. It is almost that he does not need my help. He is merely informing me of developments. He seems to know what I will approve and what I will not.' It was only a question of time before Jiten found himself being sidelined and ignored in team meetings. The dumbest, the most obedient Naradas, moved ahead of him. To Jiten, Garuda would say, 'While it is good to anticipate your master's move, it must never seem like you are one step ahead of the master. That would make you look like an oversmart upstart. Remember, your master needs to feel that you need him, that your existence and validation comes from him. Never forget that you are the cog in his wheel, he is not the cog in yours.'

Leader: 50 Insights from Mythology

21

The legacy lake

Once upon a time there was a king called Indradyumna. After a long reign he passed away and went to heaven, where he spent centuries, enjoying the rewards of his good deeds on earth. Then, one day, the gods told him, 'Indradyumna, you have to go back to earth. You are no longer welcome in heaven.'

'Why?' asked a perplexed Indradyumna. 'Because,' said the gods, 'No one on earth remembers your good deeds.' 'But how can that be?' wondered the king, 'I spent all my life doing good deeds.' 'If,' said the gods, 'you can find at least one creature who remembers you for your good deeds, you can come back to heaven. Otherwise you will have to leave. That is the rule.'

Time flows differently on earth than in heaven. When Indradyumna reached earth, he realized that centuries had passed since his reign. The trees were different, the people were different, even his kingdom looked different. Who will remember me, he wondered. The buildings he built were all gone. The temples he built were nowhere to be seen. The people who were beneficiaries of his largesse were all dead. No one he met remembered any king called Indradyumna.

Disheartened, Indradyumna went in search of the oldest man on earth. He found Rishi Markandeya. But the rishi did not remember him. 'There is an owl who is older than me,' said the sage, 'Go to him.' Markandeya did as advised. He found the owl and asked him, 'Do you remember King Indradyumna?' and the owl said, 'No, I do not remember such a king but ask the stork who is older than me.' Even the stork did not remember. 'But I know someone who is much older than me, who may know of King Indradyumna,' said the stork. 'He is an old tortoise who lives in a lake.'

Indradyumna went to the tortoise who was very old and slow and tired. But, to Indradyumna's great relief, he did remember a king called Indradyumna. 'He built this lake,' said the tortoise.

'But I never built this lake,' said Indradyumna, rather bewildered by this piece of information. 'This lake did not even exist when I was king.'

The tortoise explained, 'My grandfather never lied. He told me that this king spent his entire life giving cows in charity, hundreds of thousands of cows.' Indradyumna recollected that he had. He had been told that gifting cows assures one a place in heaven. Yes, it had, but only temporarily. Now, where were his cows? Where were the people to whom he gave the cows? The tortoise continued, 'As these cows left Indradyumna's city, they kicked up so much dust it created a depression in the ground; when the rains came water collected in this depression and turned it into a lake. Now that lake provides sustenance to innumerable plants and animals and worms and weeds and fishes and turtles and birds. So we remember the great King Indradyumna, whose act of charity resulted in a lake that for generations has been our home.'

Indradyumna was pleased to hear what the tortoise had to say. So were the gods who welcomed him back. As Indradyumna rose to heaven, the irony did not escape him: he was remembered on earth for a lake that was unconsciously created, and not for the cows that were consciously given. He benefited not from things he did, but from the impact of things he did.

This story draws attention to the notion of legacy. In ancient India, the greatest good deed that outlived anyone was go-daan or gift of a cow. In modern times, most unfortunately, this is literally translated. In a cattle-herding community, gifting cows was gift of a livelihood. But as society evolved, the phrase was carried forward to convey a different meaning. It came to mean 'gift of an opportunity'. The greatest gift a man can give another man is an opportunity that will enable the other to survive, to grow and to thrive. This could be education or a job or a loan to start a business. Gifting cows is about 'teaching a man to fish' as the Chinese proverb goes; it is not about 'giving him fish'.

During his lifetime, Arvindji built many factories and made a lot of money. Fifty years later nobody remembers how much money he made, but a large number of people remember that their fathers and mothers worked in Arvindji's factory. And because they worked in Arvindji's factory they had enough money to educate their children and their children have done well in life.

There is a hospital in Pune called Arvind Hospital. Arvindji was long dead before this hospital was built. Like Indradyumna's lake this is an unintentional consequence of his factory. The factory that he built gave livelihood to a young man who was able to raise his two sons, and he had enough money to ensure that one of the two became a doctor. The young man was always obliged to Arvindji, because before the factory was set up in the small town where he lived, he had been unemployed for over a year. It was the arrival of the factory that gave him the job. And he was eternally obliged to Arvindji for creating that opportunity. When his son built the hospital, he insisted that it be named after that 'giver of cows', Arvindji.

Often leaders plan their legacy. They say, 'Let me be remembered for this or that.' But often, it is the unintentional consequences of our deeds that are remembered. Hopefully, that unintentional consequence will be a lake, one that for centuries going forward will provide shelter and opportunity to millions.

22

Throne of generosity

 One day a king called Bhoj was passing near a field outside his city. There he observed something very peculiar. As he and his soldiers approached the field, the farmer screamed and shouted, 'Stay away, stay away, you and your horses will destroy the crops. Don't you have any pity on poor people such as me?' Surprised by the behaviour of the cantankerous farmer, Bhoj moved away. But as soon as he turned his back, the farmer changed his tune to say, 'Where are you going, my king? Please come to my field, let me water your horses and feed your soldiers. Surely, you will not say no to the hospitality of this humble farmer?'

Not wanting to hurt the farmer, though amused by his turnaround, Bhoj once again moved towards the field. Again the farmer shouted, 'Hey, go away. Your horses and your soldiers are damaging what is left of my crop. You wicked king, go away.' Bhoj once again turned away. Again the farmer changed his tunes, 'Hey, why are you turning away? Come back. You are my guests. Let me have the honour of serving you.'

Bhoj wondered what was happening. This happened a few more times. Bhoj observed the farmer carefully. He noticed that whenever the farmer was rude, he was standing on the ground. But whenever he was hospitable, he was standing on top of a mound in the middle of the field. Bhoj realized that the farmer's split personality had something to do with the mound. He immediately ordered his soldiers to dig the mound in the centre of the field. Naturally, the farmer did not like this and kept protesting. But Bhoj paid scant attention to him.

Within the mound, the soldiers found a wonderful golden throne. As Bhoj was about to sit on it, the throne spoke up, 'This is the throne of Vikramaditya the great. Sit on it only if you are as generous and wise as he was. If not, you will meet your death on the throne.' The throne then proceeded to tell Bhoj thirty-two stories of Vikramaditya, each extolling a virtue of kingship, the most important being generosity. Thus through these stories, Bhoj learnt what it takes to be a good king.

The 'thirty-two tales of Vikramaditya's throne' is part of Indian folklore. They are often condescendingly referred to as children's stories. They were never meant to entertain children; they were meant to shape the mind of future leaders. This purpose of children's stories has long been forgotten. And so, very few people notice the most interesting part of this story: What does the king's throne do to the farmer? It makes him generous. The farmer is insecure and selfish when on the ground. As soon as he is on top of the mound, he becomes generous. On the ground, he is the common man. On top of the mound, he is what a king should be.

The second part of the story is equally interesting. The throne does not let Bhoj sit on it. 'Are you as worthy and generous as Vikramaditya?' it asks through its many stories. So we are left wondering: Does the throne transform a man into a king, hence generous, or must a man first transform into a generous soul and thus become worthy of the throne? Either way, generosity seems to be the hallmark of kingship, hence leadership, at least in Indian folklore.

Animals do not give. They can only take. Through strength and cunning, they take food and shelter in order to survive. Humans, however, can give food and shelter, enabling others not only to survive but also to thrive. Thus generosity is most peculiar to humans; and the one who displays it most magnificently is recognized as king. A king or leader is 'creator of opportunities'. This fundamental reason for the existence of kings is often forgotten.

In cultural memory, kings and leaders exist for their subjects and followers. Or at least they should. They should help their subjects and followers survive and thrive. They are providers and protectors. When kings and leaders think about themselves and their glory and their dynasties, they start 'using' their subjects and followers. Kingdoms then exist for their pleasure and power. Kingdoms then are not outcomes of their kingship. Kings/leaders then become 'users of opportunity', farming the field for themselves, not for others.

A gentleman named Sundar had great friends until he became the boss of his unit. The moment he became the boss he started behaving differently, started becoming rude, obnoxious and extremely demanding. The role had changed him. The reason he gave was the burden of responsibilities. That was when Kalyana Singh, the owner of the company, decided to have a talk with him. 'Do you know why you have been given a higher salary, a car, a secretary, a cabin?' Sundar replied that they were the perks of his job. Kalyana Singh asked again, 'And what is your job?' Sundar rattled out his job description and his key result areas. 'And how do you plan to get a promotion?' Sundar replied that it would happen if he did his work diligently and reached his targets. 'No,' said Kalyana Singh, 'Absolutely not.' Sundar did not understand. Kalyana Singh explained, 'If you do your job well, why would I move you out? I will keep you exactly where you are.' Looking at the bewildered expression on Sundar's face, Kalyana Singh continued, 'If you nurture someone to take your place, then yes, I may consider promoting you. But you seem to be nurturing no one. You are too busy trying to be boss, trying to dominate people, being rude and obnoxious. That is because you are insecure. So long as you are insecure, you will not let others grow. And as long as those under you do not grow, you will not grow yourself. Or at least, I will not give you another responsibility. You will end up doing the same job forever. Do you want that?' That is the moment Sundar understood the meaning of Vikramaditya's throne.

As we go higher up the ladder, we should ideally become

more secure and hence more generous—the creators of opportunity. When this does not happen, we end up creating an organization full of cantankerous, inhospitable farmers and absolutely no kings.

23

Binding tenacity

 Savitri, the only child of king Ashwapati, fell in love with a woodcutter called Satyavan, and insisted on marrying him. But her father was against this marriage. He had good reason too. 'He is poor,' said the king. That made no difference to the love-struck princess. 'He is of fallen reputation; his father was once a king who was driven out of his kingdom,' said the father. That made no difference to the daughter. 'He is destined to die one year from now.' Even this information from the astrologers did not make any difference to Savitri. She was determined to be Satyavan's bride. Ashwapati had no choice but to give his consent, and Savitri very readily gave up all royal comforts to follow her husband to his tiny hut in the forest. After a year of bliss, Satyavan died, as foretold; Savitri saw Yama take his life away before her very eyes. Rather than accept her fate and cremate her husband's body, Savitri decided to follow the god

of death. Yama noticed the woman following him as he made his way south towards the land of the dead. The journey was long and Yama was sure Savitri would stop eventually. But she did not. Hours later, Savitri showed no signs of exhaustion. Her pursuit was relentless. 'Stop following me,' yelled Yama, but Savitri did not heed this divine command. 'Accept your fate. Go back and cremate your husband's body,' said Yama, but Savitri cared more for her husband's life breath that lay in Yama's hands than her husband's corpse that lay on the forest floor. Exasperated, Yama said, 'I give you three boons, anything but the life of your husband. Take them and go.' Savitri bowed her head respectively and for her first boon asked that her father-in-law should regain his lost kingdom. As her second boon she asked that her father be blessed with a son. As her third boon she asked that she be the mother of Satyavan's sons. Yama gave Savitri all three boons and continued on his journey to the land of the dead. Just when he reached the banks of the River Vaitarani which separates the land of the living from the land of the dead, Yama found Savitri still following him. 'I told you to take your three boons and not follow me.' Savitri once again bowed her head respectfully and said, 'The first boon has come true. My father-in-law has regained his lost kingdom. The second boon has come true. My father has a son now. But the third boon! How will it be fulfilled? How can I be mother of my husband's sons when he lies dead on the forest floor? I came to ask you that.'

Yama smiled for he realized Savitri had outwitted him. The only way his third boon could be realized was by letting

Satyavan live once again. He had no choice but to let Satyavan live. Thus Savitri was able to rewrite not only her own future but the futures of her father-in-law and father.

Had Savitri been a typical Indian, she would have simply surrendered to her father's will or to her fate. She would either have not married Satyavan or she would have accepted widowhood without any resistance. At least that is what we are led to believe is the Indian way. But Savitri defied all things: she refused to accept her father's will or her fate. She made her own decision and stuck to it—and was so determined to have her way that she subverted even the laws of nature, by a judicious use of desire, determination, shrewdness and selflessness.

Like Savitri, Gille knows the value of desire. Four years ago, Gille was a cycle mechanic. Today, he has his own shop and he also rents the place out to a tea vendor for extra income. This was unimaginable four years ago when he came to Delhi and was not given any shelter by his relatives or his friends. Homeless, with barely fifty rupees in his pocket, he refused to surrender to the odds before him. His tenacity stemmed from desire. He wanted to make it big—he wanted to achieve something in life. His desire, he realized, was the root of all his actions. Like Savitri, who wanted Satyavan, he wanted something. Unless there is desire there can be no action. But desire alone is not enough. It had to be translated into determination. Come what may, he would not let go of his dreams. Like Savitri, who followed Yama, he pursued his dream: went from shop to shop looking for a job. He did not let rejection lead to dejection. He just continued looking for a job and found one—no pay, just a place to stay and two meals a day. This was exploitation, he knew, but it was better than nothing. It was a start. This job gave Gille many opportunities. And he used this opportunity not to help only himself. Like Savitri, who first helped her father-in-law and then her father, he went out of his way to help those around him, thereby earning great equity and making great friends. All this provided him the support that helped him save his meager earnings first and then set up his own cycle shop. He gave his best friend an opportunity to open a tea stall thereby becoming independent himself. Like Savitri who outwitted Yama by not directly asking for Satyavan's life, but indirectly doing so by asking for sons by her husband, Gille was shrewd. He knew the ways of the world and was smart in using favours. Like getting his former boss to partner with him, offering to work for free just to get the initial capital for his cycle shop. Once the business boomed, he made more than enough to buy out his partner and become full owner of the cycle shop. It is only a question of time before Gille does better. He has the wisdom of Savitri. During the festival of Savitri, women go around banyan trees with a string. Banyan trees are symbols of permanence. By binding this symbol with a string, the women are ritually expressing their 'permanent' desire and determination for a good home. All leaders who 'get things done' need to bind their desires to the tree of permanence so that like Savitri, through desire, determination, selflessness and shrewdness, they can and will give shape to their thought, no matter what.

24

The poison of stagnation

Last Sunday, Shivkumar got transfer orders and he is upset. For years he has served the company loyally, not taken a single day's leave, made it to office even when he had fever. Never late to office, he has worked diligently, doing all his work, even that of others, staying back in office every day, leaving only after his boss had left, making sure that all is in order. All his life he had stayed in Lucknow, in his family house. He walked to work and enjoyed the neighbourhood. Now this! How could they do this to him? How could they transfer him to Allahabad? Yes, the new office needed setting up, but why him? Surely, they could send someone junior, or someone more experienced in setting up new offices? He had not taken a promotion so that he could stay here. He was willing to take a pay cut to stay here. He just did not want to go to Allahabad. But this new boss, the one who came from Delhi, is a scoundrel. He just will not listen. 'You must go to Allahabad, Shivkumarji. The company needs you to do this. And I need you to do this. And it is for your own good.' Your own good? How can it be for his good? Moving to a new place, a new neighbourhood, a new house, the headache of school admissions, the pain of shifting furniture. And who would look after his family house while he was away? And his parents? Would they also have to move? His mother would never agree.

Shivkumar does not know this. But he is what Kaliya had become to Yamuna—poisonous. There was a bend in the river Yamuna near Vrindavan that was shunned by all the cowherds and cows. The water there was lethal. Even a blade of grass that fell into these waters shrivelled in an instant. This was the result of the poison that a great serpent called Kaliya spat out each day. When Krishna learnt of this, he decided to tackle the serpent. 'Don't!' shouted his friends, but Krishna would hear none of it. He jumped into the river and began splashing about in glee, laughing at his friends who stood on the river banks begging him to come back. The disturbance caused Kaliya to stir and rise up from the river bed. He sprang up and grabbed Krishna in his coils. He spread his hood and prepared to strike the young lad, but to his astonishment, Krishna turned out to be a nimble fighter, slipping out of his coils with ease and striking him hard on his hood. Before Kaliya could react, Krishna had leapt on his hood and was dancing on it. No, that was no dance; he was being kicked into submission. 'Go, go, go,' Krishna said. Kaliya resisted. He thrashed about, swung his tail like the trunk of an elephant and shook his hood. He hissed and he bared his fangs, he twisted and turned, rose up and went down the water, determined to shake Krishna off. But Krishna stood firm on his hood and grabbed his tail. He kept kicking Kaliya's head, shouting, 'Go, go, go.' Kaliya refused. 'Why?' asked Krishna in a voice that was kind but firm. 'Because,' said Kaliya, 'I am afraid. Beyond this bend lurks the hawk, Garuda. I am terrified of him. If he sees me, he will swoop down from the skies and grab me by his talons and make a meal out of me. Here, I am unseen. Here, I am safe.' Krishna smiled and said, 'Life is about movement, not stagnation. You cannot let fear paralyse you. The more you stay here, the more you poison the waters. Go, don't be afraid. Have faith. You will survive. Just move. You will find a way to outwit Garuda and overcome your fear of him. You will. Trust me.'

In images, Kaliya, the serpent, is shown with a hood. A Cobra spreads its hood only when it is stationary. When it is mobile it does not have a hood. The hooded Kaliya thus represents stillness. When Kaliya refuses to move, the water around him becomes poisonous. This clearly is a metaphor for one's refusal to change out of fear—the refusal to move out of the zone of comfort, because exploration of the unknown terrifies us. Kaliya is terrified of Garuda. Garuda is at once a real fear and an imagined fear. Garuda is the bottleneck to Kaliya's movement, to Kaliya's growth, to Kaliya's conquest of his own insecurity. What seems like punishment to Kaliya, is actually a lesson in wisdom. 'Go,' says Krishna, 'move on, face life, don't hide. Swim in the river as you are supposed to. The more you hide, the more you harm yourself and others around you.'

Shivkumar believes his boss from Delhi is Kaliya who needs to be kicked back by Krishna. But in fact, he is the Kaliya. His boss has recognized his potential—his ability to contribute so much more, not just to the organization but also to himself. Shivakumar short sells himself, even to himself. He hides behind apparent contentment. Yet, he is envious of the young ones in the company who have been promoted and who have been given better bonuses and incentives. He resents other people's success. He wants success to come to him—but he refuses to change anything in his life. He will not compromise on his routines, in his working style, in his dealings with people. He likes things to stay the way they are. He gets angry when friends move on to other cities, to other jobs. He gets upset when bosses accept transfers, when the houses in the neighbourhood are broken down to make way for new structures. He loves telling all those who are willing to hear, 'Those were the days!'

Things are changing every day around Shivkumar. But Shivkumar is refusing to adapt. Before him is an opportunity to experience something new. A transfer, a new city, a new job, new friends, new opportunities. But he is afraid. Garuda lurks beyond the bend of his river. He is angry with Krishna. He does not want to go. But Krishna's dance will not stop. The transfer order will not be revoked, and he will be told, 'Go, go, go.'

25

The ultimate alpha male

 In ancient India, the throne on which kings sat was known as the Singh-asan, the lion-seat. The patron goddess of kings, Durga, also rode lions. Images of lions adorned the gates of royal palaces and could be seen atop pillars. One such image adorns our national emblem. The close association of lions with royalty had a reason. Everyone knew that the lion was the king of the jungle, the greatest predator, on top of the food chain with no natural enemy. But that was not what a king was supposed to be.

Lions are the ultimate alpha males. A lion lays claim over a pride of lionesses by fighting off other males. The battle is fierce. The winner takes it all. The losers are left without mates. There is no sharing. When a lion takes over a pride it kills all the cubs fathered by the previous alpha male. Thus he ensures that only his gene pool survives. Having taken over a pride, he rests, leaving all the hunting to the lionesses. When the lionesses hunt a prey, they make way and allow the lion to eat his fill before they feed themselves. Thus in a pride, the lionesses do all the work while the lion enjoys the fruits of their labour. They hunt, he eats. They bear his cubs and take care of the young, it is the lion who decides if a young cub should live or die. He is the absolute master and they are his slaves.

For many people, lions are the perfect symbol of leadership. Followers should be like lionesses, afraid of and subservient to the lion. When the leader takes over he wipes out all traces of the predecessor. The leader does no work, nor does he help or guide. All he does is relax and stake claim to the fruits of the labour of the followers.

This is the case in the warehouse at Bhiwandi where Shekhawat is in charge. He sits all day in his office and expects his team to deliver. If they don't, he denies them wages or delays their bonuses. Everybody fears Shekhawat. There are rumours that he uses violence to intimidate his people. He does not like being criticized. And if anyone complains about him to the management, they risk losing their job or something worse. But the management in Mumbai allows Shekhawat to function. He is their iron man. They feel only he can manage the rather tough lot at the warehouse. Before Shekhawat, they had sent Pande to manage the warehouse. Pande was a gentleman who tried to motivate the men with words and tried to get everyone to follow the policies. But the labourers were a rowdy bunch. They simply ignored Pande and threatened to form a union when he tried to act tough. Pande had to be replaced. Shekhawat was brought in. He used brute force to get the workers at the warehouse in order. They quivered in his presence. Like lionesses, they did what he told them to do. This made the management happy. But they are also afraid. Shekhawat knows his power and is slowly becoming a law unto himself. There are rumours that he demands bribes from vendors before allowing their goods to be unloaded from trucks. No one is sure, but no one is willing to check. They fear the roar of Shekhawat.

Shekhawat is practising leadership by fear. He is the lion. His team makes up his lionesses. The tragedy is, as observed in the case of Pande, his followers respond only to a lion. They want to be lionesses!

Leadership by fear may not be part of management books, but it a tried and tested method. Feudalism is essentially leadership by fear. Today explicit violence may be considered illegal and uncivilized, but implicit violence is still practised, and extremely popular. The most popular non-violent fear-inducing tool is the threat of sacking people. This is especially visible when the markets are down and jobs are scarce. When a manager says, 'My way or the high way,' it is a lion growling. One often hears managers moaning that young people today are not afraid and in fact threaten to quit when threatened with sacking, indicating their desire to be lions.

But in ancient India, the king was expected to sit on a lion, not be a lion. His patron goddess, Durga, rode a lion, meaning she domesticated the king of the jungle. The message here is about human beings having the ability to overpower and outgrow the animal urge to dominate and frighten others into submission. The king was not expected to treat his people like animals who needed to be controlled by fear or force, or tamed by 'carrot and stick'. To treat people like lionesses and to behave like a lion is an act of dehumanization. A king was expected to help his subjects discover their humanity. Humans are the only animals who can empathize. The king was therefore expected to provoke his people into empathy, and in the process unlock their own hidden potential. To be the lion is to be the leader who frightens. To sit on the lion-throne is to be a leader who inspires.

26

Talking matters

 It is said that when Vyasa narrated the epic Mahabharata, the elephant-headed Ganesha served as his scribe and, using his tusk as his pen, wrote the epic on palm leaf manuscripts. But who read this book? Mahabharata typically comes to us, not in the form of a book, but as a narration made by Sauti, the bard, to Shaunaka, the sage, in the Naimisha forest. Sauti heard the tale from his father who in turn heard it from Vaishampayana, who narrated it at the great snake sacrifice of Janamejaya, king of Hastinapur. Vaishamapayana had learnt the tale from Vyasa, his teacher. This preference for the 'spoken word' over the 'written word' in the mythological realm is a reflection of Indian psyche. Indians prefer to say things, and hear things, rather than read things or write them down.

Even the Vedas, the collection of mantras that contain the most primal of Hindu thoughts, are said to be *Shruti*—that which was heard. Revelation came to the Rishis in the form of a divine whisper: an auditory communication. Contrast this with the Biblical tradition where God communicated his commandments in the form of ten laws written on two stone tablets that Moses brought down from Mount Sinai. There is clearly an articulation of the cultural difference in matters of communication.

A French student witnessed this when he decided to do his internship in an Indian software company. He observed that his colleagues resisted writing down minutes of the meeting or preparing a project plan with clear milestones and roles and responsibilities. Yet, everyone seemed to know their duties and their deadlines. He noticed that the requirements of the clients went through many changes. A lot was discussed over the telephone but hardly anything was written. Everything was in the 'head' of the engineers and the 'head' of the clients. To his surprise, the software was developed on schedule. No attempt was made by the client to reconcile the requirement documents with what was finally delivered. What mattered to the client was that the new system worked! The French intern also noticed that the user manual had many discrepancies—the screen shots were older versions, there were many grammatical errors. This did not bother the client; he suspected the client had not seen the manual. All the users on the client side insisted on demonstrations. But the training was not very detailed. A colleague explained, 'They will keep calling us when they face problems for the next couple of months.' The intern realized such casual calls were an unwritten part of the contract that ensured a good relationship with the client and brought repeat business.

Historians have noticed that compared to their counterparts in China, Greece and Arabia, Indians have been rather poor chroniclers. Referring to law books constantly to check if social behaviour is appropriate is a relatively new phenomenon, a legacy that came with British rule. Unlike the Bible or the Koran, no particular book has anchored the religious beliefs and practices of the Hindus. Even today, for spiritual training, one is advised to approach a guru, a living, breathing person, rather than a book.

Some say that the Indian obsession with the spoken word may have something to do with the fact that most people in India are illiterate. Reading and writing was restricted only to men belonging to certain castes for centuries. But this was the case in most cultures around the world. Despite rising literacy in modern India, the preference for the spoken word remains. Hence wedding cards are always delivered in person or at least followed up by a telephone call. More than the card, it is the visit and the telephone that makes people feel truly invited and included. The same applies to business communication.

Good leaders in India never rely on written communication to get work done from their team. Just an email message will not work. If things have to move, he has to pick up the phone and talk to each and every member. And if it is really serious then he must go to them personally and talk it out in detail. Verbal communication is the key to success in the Indian business environment.

It has been argued that the Indian preference for the 'spoken word' has something to do with the fact that Indians are a highly emotional people, and the written word, with its commas, semicolons and bullet points, is dry and crisp, unable to communicate feelings. As one speaks, one is able to communicate through intonations, body language and facial expressions many things beyond what is being actually said. By speaking, one can connect emotionally.

Others say that Indians are more comfortable with the spoken word because unlike the written word, the spoken word cannot be carved in stone. Truth is India is not permanent; it is contextual, depending on space and time and mood. What was OK yesterday may not be OK today. There is a sense of finality in the written word which is not there with the spoken word. The spoken word seems more flexible, making room for unforeseen situations that may emerge.

Indians write only when something is serious or final—a memo, an application for leave, a business contract, a memorandum of agreement, an application or termination letter, an urgent telegram. Until then, the mode of communication remains speech. The booming telecom industry is proof that Indians love to talk.

A good leader must ask himself how many times and how much time in a day does he spend talking to his team and to his customers. Then he must ask how many times does he approach them and how many times do they approach him. This is the measure of successful communication. It is also important to see how much of the conversation is functional and task-motivated and how much is personal and emotion-motivated. It is also important for the leader to let his team speak more—so that he can be sure that he has been heard and understood, and also to discover what lies in the heart and soul of his team, what really matters to them. It is the latter chit-chat about friends, families, aspirations, fears, office gossip and relationship politics that ultimately serves as the glue to a powerful team.

27

Narada on the prowl

 Randhir was very happy with his bonus until someone told him that his colleague, Sukant, had been given a higher bonus. 'It's not fair,' he said and stormed to meet his boss. Despite every attempt of his boss to explain his evaluation logically, Randhir remained convinced that his boss prefers Sukant because Sukant is a 'yes-man'. He is hurt at not being the 'chosen one' of the boss. And he carries this pain everywhere he goes—sharing it with friends after the first glass of whisky, sharing it with his wife as soon as he reaches home.

The same thing has happened to Kartikeya, a god. His father, Shiva, an ascetic who is usually indifferent to worldly things, gave a mango to his brother, Ganesha, not to him. The mango was supposed to be given to Shiva's 'better son'. Kartikeya rejected the evaluation method used by his father.

He was so angry at being less preferred, that he moved out of his father's house, so say the scriptures.

Who gave Shiva the mango for the better son? Who told Randhir that Sukant was given a higher bonus?

It was Narada, a lute-wielding sage who wanders from place to place spreading gossip and making mischief, always announcing his arrival and departure by chanting the name of God, 'Narayana, Narayana.'

The story goes that Narada was amongst the first creations of Brahma. He was a mind-born son, moulded out of Brahma's thoughts, making him an extremely enlightened creation. He observed the world that his father was creating and noticed it was restless and eternally transforming, going through endless cyclical changes. He concluded it was a meaningless merry-go-round. So he went around telling all of Brahma's creations, 'This world does not matter. You do not matter. Everything changes eventually so nothing really matters.' Hearing him, all living creatures lost their motivation to grow. Leaves wilted and animals wasted away. Humans refused to marry and produce children. Everyone agreed with Narada that the whole exercise of living life and populating the world was rather pointless. 'Let us all sit and meditate and become one with the absolute eternal truth,' said Narada, and everyone followed him, much to Brahma's dismay. A furious Brahma cursed Narada. 'May you be eternally restless, may you move without pause from one end of this material world to another, making everyone you meet see the value of creation.' Narada bowed his head and surrendered to the curse. He would travel.

Leader: 50 Insights from Mythology

And he would show the value of the world. But not quite what the way the creator had in mind.

Narada went to Shiva and offered him a mango saying, 'It is for your "better" son.' That statement made the mango very valuable. And it compelled Shiva to choose between his two sons: Ganesha and Kartikeya. Before Shiva could begin his evaluation, he could feel the tension in his family. His two sons looked at him with eyes full of expectation and his wife watched from the corner, tapping her feet, wondering whether his decision would be the same as hers. Suddenly, the peace of Shiva's life was shattered. Value had been created. Judgements had to be made. And whatever the judgements, there would be repercussions, for not everyone will see things the same way.

Bound by his father's curse, Narada then moved to another location, followed by another, and another, sharing evaluations, provoking evaluations, drawing attention to the value of Brahma's world. Evaluations are followed by judgements, and with judgements come choices, with choices come emotions. Narada's intervention typically evokes negative emotions. The material world, once dismissed by Narada himself as a mirage, now becomes so meaningful that there is anger, jealously, outrage—a desire to fight, to strike back, to teach the world a lesson, to pull contenders down, push competitors behind, until the evaluation gets done in one's favour.

Narada continues to be on the prowl ... Step into any organization anywhere in the world, and if you find 'office politics' know that Narada has been at work. You can sense his presence at almost every office lunch or late-night booze party, where invariably, inevitably, someone will provide fodder for enthusiastic conversations about cunning secretaries, unfair promotions, manipulative colleagues, favouritism of bosses, disproportionate salaries and nefarious practices.

The Narada phenomenon is universal, not just in the corporate world. It can be seen in playgrounds, in building societies, in temple committees, amongst grandchildren and grandparents, amongst the educated and the illiterate, in Ekta Kapur serials as well as Satyajit Ray movies, amongst the richest of the rich and the poorest of the poor, reminding us that Narada has clearly taken his curse very seriously.

But while it is easy to blame Narada for the tensions in our lives and for the unending crookedness that is celebrated in soap operas, we forget that we are as much the topic of Narada's conversation as the recipient of it, the victims and the victimizers. Wherefrom comes the need to indulge in office politics? Does it come from our need to compare? Wherefrom comes our need to be evaluated correctly by the world around us? Is that what is provoking us to struggle and strive in our personal and professional lives—our uncertainty about our self-worth? Would we listen to Narada if we were self-contained?

Logically speaking, we have the capacity to ignore that information. But we don't. We are eager to believe gossip. We are eager to believe the worst of others. We are eager to surrender to negative emotions. Peace is boring. Relentless happiness does not make a good story. So we literally invite

Narada into our lives, into our homes and offices. We encourage him to give us fodder to stir us into righteous outrage. And he obliges.

And as we bicker and bitch, Narada watches from the shadows, waiting when the world will be exhausted of these petty emotions and focus on something more meaningful. Is he, in a convoluted way, asking us to have a little faith in ourselves and focus less on what the world thinks of us and more what we can do for the world? Why else would he intersperse all his gossip with 'Narayana, Narayana,' (his name for God) all the time? Notice, how of all words that leaves Narada's lips, these two are the least heard.

28

Different drum

According to the *Shiva Purana,* Daksha-Prajapati sought worthy grooms for his many daughters, men of substance, gods who helped life on earth, like Indra the rain-god or Agni, the fire-god. He was quite horrified therefore when his youngest daughter, Sati, of her own free will, chose a hermit as a husband—a naked, ash-smeared ascetic called Shiva who had dogs and ghosts as his companions and who lived atop a snow-clad mountain. Upset that his daughter had married against his will, and that too a person so unconventional, he severed all relations with her. When he decided to perform a grand yagna, he invited all his daughters and sons-in-law to the ceremony, but not Shiva or Sati.

Many of us in the corporate world are Daksha-Prajapatis, who in our eagerness to create collaborative working environments that work towards the corporate goal, include in our teams only 'appropriate grooms'—people whose energies match ours and who align to our way of working. We do not willingly let a Shiva in—the maverick, the iconoclast, the one who thinks differently, who seems condescending, cold, distant … even bizarre.

Daksha-Prajapati rejected Shiva because Shiva did not fit his definition of a god. Shiva can easily be misunderstood for a contrarian, people who oppose for the sake of opposing or for a rebel or for an attention seeker, someone who thinks he is too good to align with an existing way of being. The fact is a Shiva simply marches to the beat of a different drummer. When he walks around smeared with ash, he is not mocking the gold-bedecked, silk-clad Vishnu. He is indifferent to worldly parameters of appropriateness.

The story goes that when Daksha-Prajapati refused to invite Shiva to his yagna, Sati flew into such a rage that she burnt herself to death in protest and disrupted the entire ceremony. A great confrontation followed where Daksha-Prajpati and his guests saw the fury and power of Shiva. An uneasy peace was finally restored, with Daksha-Prajapati begging for forgiveness and Shiva withdrawing into his cave. No one was in doubt of Shiva's might anymore but it seemed too explosive to handle.

It is only in crisis that the value of a Shiva is realized. Crisis emerges when conventional ways of working and assumed solutions fail to deliver. When problems turn out to be out of the ordinary, we need unconventional thinking: we need a Shiva. A Shiva is the kind of person who can bring a fresh new perspective. He may innovate but not deliver. He may not be as tuned as an entrepreneur to the value of his wisdom; or he may simply find the process of convincing others of the solution too much of a bother.

A crisis arose when the demon king Taraka assumed power; the gods with all their conventional weapons were unable to destroy him. A warlord was needed, one who was fathered by Shiva. But before Shiva could father this great warrior, he had to be enchanted by a woman. For that the gods had to make him open his eyes. So they used the standard solution: Kama, god of lust, was asked to shoot the arrow of desire into Shiva's heart. The plan backfired. Shiva found the effects of the arrow a disturbance; he simply opened his third eye and set Kama aflame.

Many of us believe that we can recruit anyone into the team with promises of great pay packets and pompous designations. But such transactions do not work with a Shiva, he does not need money, he does not need his ego to be propped with high-flying titles. That is what is most exasperating about a Shiva. He does not subscribe to any conventional pattern of thinking. To get him on board one needs a different approach.

The gods turned to Goddess Shakti, who took birth as Gauri, a mountain princess. She connected with Shiva not by arousing his senses or appeasing his ego, but by simply demonstrating her determination: she meditated on him without eating or sleeping, forcing him to appear before her. She then appealed to his compassion and surrendered to his wisdom. 'Marry me,' she said. He agreed, not even knowing what being a husband means, such was his indifference to worldly ways. As wife, Gauri slowly initiated Shiva in the ways of the householder, gradually unlocking his power for the benefit of the world. Thanks to her, the gods got the divine warlord Kartikeya who helped them destroy Taraka.

With Gauri by his side, Shiva became Shankara. While as Shiva, he was silent and still, with both eyes firmly shut, as Shankara, he spoke and danced, and opened his eyes. He heard the cries of his devotees and responded to them. He became the benevolent easy-to-please boon giver. He was no longer distant.

Gauri realized that while many people followed Shiva, he was no leader. He could not be expected to collaborate with the team or motivate people or drive them towards a goal. He was raw energy, neither positive nor negative, with no opinion either way. Realizing this demons like Ravana exploited both his power and his innocence until Gauri came along.

Gauri succeeded where Daksha-Prajapati and Kama had failed. Daksha-Prajapati is the authoritarian who demands alignment to a system. Kama is a friend, an enchanter, a charmer, who convinces you to willingly become part of the system. Gauri realized that seducing Shiva into a system by force would only lead to disaster; eventually he would withdraw or create havoc. Therefore, even though she was his wife, she allowed Shiva to remain the wandering mendicant he was. Without changing his core personality, she was able to channel his genius for the benefit of the world through understanding, determination, perseverance and intelligence.

Perhaps in a way, we are all Shiva—individualists, creative thinkers, who function best when allowed to be ourselves. Over time we all become Shankaras, gradually getting drawn into the system, connecting and working with others, becoming part of teams and common visions. Some Shankaras even become Vishnus—totally assimilated to the ways of the world. A good CEO who knows the value of diversity, needs to ensure that his organization has the whole range of people—many Vishnus, a large number of Shankaras and a few Shivas.

29

Monkey leaders and cat leaders

Akbar, the greatest of the Mughals, was addressed as Jahanpanah. The word means 'Shelter of the world'. Was it a title meant to boost the ego of the great emperor of India? Or did it contain the people's expectation from their leader?

A leader is supposed to be the 'shelter'—protector, defender, the one who creates the environment where one can thrive. He is supposed to provide physical shelter, intellectual shelter, emotional shelter and economic shelter. He is supposed to help you become a better person. Now, that is a huge responsibility on a leader. Leadership then becomes not just a functional role; it becomes a deeply spiritual one, because it demands one to draw out the best in one's followers. Leadership is then an exercise, not in power, but in love, where power is but a medium.

When Sarita joined an animation studio, she was surprised to find a boss like Tulika who spent hours with her trying to find out what motivated her, what excited her, and giving her work that both challenged and excited her. Sarita felt she mattered and gave her best to Tulika.

Sarita felt that Tulika was a better boss than Prithvi, her previous boss. She felt Prithvi ignored her, never really spent time with her, in fact was quite indifferent to her. But was he?

Prithvi's style of management was clearly different from Tulika's. Like Tulika, Prithvi deeply cared for Sarita's well-being—but he was not that obvious. He ensured that Sarita only got work that brought out the best for her. He never let the rest of the organization take advantage of his team. He shielded his team from office politics and ensured they worked regular hours and did not stay back late. When Sarita came to him he answered all her queries and taught her a few more skills. He was never angry when she made mistakes. In fact, in company meetings, he held himself responsible for all his team's shortcomings and gave them full credit for all successes.

Prithvi was a more reactive boss. Tulika was more proactive. But both were, without being aware of it, serving as 'shelters' to their respective teams. Who is better, the proactive boss or the reactive boss? The former seems more emotional and caring. The latter seems distant, even indifferent, but is always available in times of crisis.

Similar thoughts emerged in south India, in the eleventh century, as acharyas such as Ramanuja were transforming the abstract and highly intellectual Vedanta philosophy into a more concrete and emotional bhakti or devotional path. They wondered what the ideal relationship should be between the deity and devotee. Everyone agreed that God is the shelter of the devotee but how must one behave before God or rather what must one expect from God?

Two schools of thought emerged. One school was the cat-school, which said God is like a cat and so devotees must be like kittens. The kitten just surrenders itself to its mother and the mother holds it by the scruff of its neck and takes it to safety. The other school was the monkey school, which said God is like a monkey and so devotees must cling to God as baby monkeys cling to their mothers. One must not let go. In the cat school, God makes all the effort, the devotee simply lets go. In the monkey school, the devotee makes all the effort, God is always present, ready to help if asked for it.

In Sarita's case, Tulika is clearly of the cat school of leadership while Prithvi is from the monkey school of leadership. For centuries people have argued which school is superior. Leaders have to choose which school suits their personality best. Are they proactive shelter providers like cats or are they reactive shelter providers like monkeys?

Problems start when the team is made of kittens but the leader is like a monkey or vice versa. One's expectation from the leader will never be met. Clinging to the cat is not advisable and hoping the monkey will carry you to safety will never happen. So the leader—follower relationship, like the deity—devotee relationship, can be complex, changing with context.

Equating the leader with the divine may seem blasphemous to many. But since ancient times, leaders, and especially kings, have always been placed on a pedestal, higher than man but lower than God. This was seen in Egypt, where the pharaoh was called the god king. In France, he was called the sun king, the temporal representative of God, around whom the world moved. The king was the closest physical manifestation the common man had to God. That is why there were elaborate ceremonies associated with their ascension to the throne. The rituals elevated the man towards the heavens, after which he was expected to become less human and more divine, thinking less about his own pleasures and more about the happiness of others. In other words, rituals were supposed to make him Jahanpanah. His sphere of influence and concern extended beyond his family and friends to include everyone within his jurisdiction and even beyond.

When Shivaji was crowned king, he was given the title of Chatrapati—lord of the parasol, the one who holds the umbrella. For whom was the king supposed to hold the umbrella? For the people, to shelter them from the relentless rain of problems. Some kings run after their children with the umbrella, when the rains fall, for they follow the cat-school of leadership. Others hold the umbrella up and wait for the children to gather around them when the rains come, for they follow the monkey school of leadership.

Leader: 50 Insights from Mythology

30

When nobody cares

Sandeep has got his pink slip today. He is shattered. He has worked very hard for three years. Suddenly, the market is down, the company is not doing so well, and he is left without a job. How will he pay his bills now? How will he repay his loans through EMIs (equilibrated monthly instalments)? What will he do?

He went to his boss. The boss said, 'The management said that I don't need a ten-member team; I can do with seven. So I was asked to give pink slips to three.' 'Why me?' Sandeep demanded. The boss explained, 'We looked at your previous year's appraisal and you were second lowest, so I had to let you go. I am sorry.' Sandeep shouted, 'You said that this appraisal business is all humbug, that you really don't believe in it. You only said that it was a process and as far as you were concerned, it was just a tick mark. I believed you. And now it has cost me my job.' 'I am sorry,' said his boss, refusing to meet his eye.

Sandeep's boss did not tell him something—of that managers meeting where everyone made a list of their favourites and then found reasons to put the rest on the chopping block. The method of chopping—appraisal scores in some cases, insubordination in some other—did not matter to the management. What mattered was the reduction in headcount. Costs had to be brought down.

The CFO does not know Sandeep's name. For him Sandeep is but a statistic. He told his CEO, 'We cannot pay all of them, so let's reduce headcount from 120 to 110 or maybe 100.' The CEO said, 'Maybe there is another option; we can reduce the salaries of the top management.' The CFO glared at the CEO and said, 'You can reduce your salary but not mine.' None of the management was willing to cut their salary; so jobs had to go to reduce cost. Reasons were elaborately created to justify the pink slip. Now Sandeep has to fend for himself. He has no one's patronage. He is no one's favourite. He is a man without a leader.

Sandeep's story has been told in the Mahabharata long ago. His name was Sunahshepa then.

One of the several versions of the story goes that there was a king, sometime identified as Harishchandra and sometime identified as Ambarisha, who had an attack of dropsy—his body swelled up with fluid. He prayed to Varuna, god of water, and said, 'If I am cured, I will sacrifice my son.' As soon as he said this, he was cured. His limbs became normal. His fingers and face were no longer bloated. 'My sacrifice?' asked Varuna. Now that he was cured, the king found it hard to part with his son. So he called the wise men of his kingdom, and told them to find a way out. 'How can I make Varuna happy without losing my son?' he asked.

The wise men said a son is defined in many ways according to the scriptures: one is the son you produce biologically, another is the son who is adopted and, finally, there is another son that you can buy. Hearing this the king said, 'Go buy me a son.' The wise men went around the kingdom, but no man was willing to sell his son. How can our king ask us to part with a son, they wondered. Who would do such a thing?

After a long search, the wise men found a poor priest willing to sell his son for a 100 cows. His name was Ajigarta. He said, 'I have three sons. I will not sell my eldest son because he is very dear to me, and I cannot sell the youngest because he is dear to his mother. I will sell my middle son, Sunahshepa, because I have no choice. I am very poor and I need to feed my family.'

Thus, Sunahshepa became the son of the king and was brought to the palace on a golden palanquin. He was quite excited until, after being fed and clothed and given gifts meant for princes, he was taken and tied to a sacrificial post. 'You, Sunahshepa, are to be sacrificed to Varuna so that your father, the king, is free of debt,' said the wise men. Realizing his hopeless situation, Sunahshepa began to cry.

The executioner was called to sacrifice the boy. 'I will not sacrifice the boy, he is no criminal,' said the executioner. The butcher was called to sacrifice the boy. 'I will not sacrifice the boy, he is no animal,' said the butcher. The priests were told to sacrifice the boy. 'We will not sacrifice the boy. That is not part of our responsibilities,' said the priests. Suddenly, a voice rang across the sacrificial hall, 'I will. I will. For 100 more cows.' It was Ajigarta, Sunahshepa's father!

Everybody was aghast and looked at the father, and said, 'When you sold your son, your reason was poverty. What is your reason now?' 'Why should I feel ashamed,' said Ajigarta, 'When the king is not ashamed to sacrifice one of his subjects to save his son.'

Watching his father move towards the chopping block, axe in hand, Sunahshepa realized he had no one he could turn to, neither father nor king. In despair, he raised his head and sang prayers, begging for divine intervention. The scriptures say, Varuna was moved by the prayers. He saved the boy, cured the king and all ended well. But did it actually?

There are many Sunahshepas in the corporate world—victims of greed, stripped of livelihood because someone wants to protect favourites, someone wants reduction in head-count and no one wants reduction in salary. Sunahshepas are created when leaders refuse to make sacrifices.

31

The palki

Imagine a palki, or palanquin, and those carrying it. It's a good symbolic representation of a team or an organization. The leader sits on it and wants his followers to take him where he wants to go. He gives the directions. He gives the motivation. He gives the reward. The followers carry him around. He is the head and they are the arms and legs. This is the classical model of leadership, popular among many.

The opposite is also true. Those who glamourize the 'servant-leadership' model often imagine the leader carrying the team on his shoulders or on his head, enabling them to reach their goals. This romantic model is essentially a reversal of the power structure assumed in a classical organization but rarely presented so.

These models work on the assumption that workers don't

think—they just do. Even in a knowledge economy, what matters is the task and output of the worker, which are measureable. These models function very well on the physical plane, where behaviour can be measured.

But there is another plane in which people function: the psychological plane, where anything is possible. You can carry the palanquin and still disobey the boss. You can make the boss carry you and still feel he is in charge. And this is what happens in most organizations.

This is especially true in India, where since ancient times, great value has been placed on the psychological plane (manas in Sanskrit). Western management models, based on Abrahamic and Greek mythology, which are highly behavioural in nature, find this psychological approach highly disconcerting as it defies control and seems to be perennially disconcerting. In fact, all union problems and acts of subversion in organizations emerge only in the psychological plane. It is the invisible root cause.

Let's take the case of Nahusha. He asked seven sages to carry him on a palanquin to the abode of his queen. They agreed reluctantly, out of respect for his kingship though they felt this was not the way to treat a sage. They were philosophers, not labourers.

On the way, Nahusha became impatient as the sages were moving very slowly. He noticed that the short sage Agastya was slowing the pace. So he kicked Agastya on his head and asked him to move faster. An angry Agastya cursed Nahusha: 'May you turn into a snake and carry yourself on your own belly.' Nahusha immediately turned into a snake, no longer carried by sages, but carrying himself on his own belly. The story shows the power of the palanquin-bearers and how they can subvert the process if they so wish.

Subverting bosses on a psychological plane is rather easy. Method 1 involves agreeing with them and doing your own thing; often the boss forgets to follow up and even forgets what he had asked. Method 2 is pretending not to understand. This forces the boss to continuously edit his comments and simplify them until what he says is what you understand, or rather, what you want to do. In the first method, there is defiance, hence the danger of retribution. In the second method, the boss feels good about himself, not realizing that he has been duped.

Nahusha managed to get the sages to serve him as palanquin-bearers and he would have surely reached his destination had he not been impatient and tried to control them. Leaders must never forget that they are riding a palanquin borne by employees. The relationship is fragile and delicate. Too much of screaming and you may end up cursed. And if you try to be too nice, you may end up carrying them on your head and feeling good about yourself as the 'servant leader.'

32

Wooing the right way

This was the agenda: to get Shiva married. It was important for unless this happened the world would be destroyed. How does one get an ascetic like Shiva to change his mind?

This question is no different from asking: How do we get a consumer to buy our product or how do we get our employee to stick to our company? Every customer—external or internal—is actually Shiva, with the power to destroy us through indifference. How do we get them to open their eyes? Not the third eye of detachment, but the two eyes of interest.

The most common approach is the Kama approach. Kama is the god of love who shoots arrows that will spawn desire in the heart of hermits. Kama seduces rishis like Vishwamitra with apsaras like Menaka. This approach means stirring the most primal instincts of man—hunger, greed, lust.

Chang, the new marketing head of a global pharma company, saw the popularity of the Kama approach amongst most of the new hopefuls he was interviewing for the position of brand manager. When asked how to increase market share, the reply was invariably, 'By lowering the price.' When asked how to motivate the sales force, the most common response was, 'By giving them better incentives.' In other words, most of those being interviewed were applying their levers to the wallet. They did not, or could not, think beyond transaction.

The Kama approach works when one visualizes the customer as a rishi who aspires to be a deva, constantly craving for the next best deal. Shoot one arrow, get one apsara to do her dance, offer instant gratification, lower prices, hike incentives, and boom! you have success. Instant consumer conversion! Instant employee satisfaction!

But for how long? Sooner or later there will be another apsara in the market, a competitor offering a lower price or a higher pay packet. The rishi who was seduced by one can easily be seduced by another. Lust can never create loyalty.

In the Kamakshi approach, we visualize the target not as deva, a common god, but as Maha-deva, God, with a capital G. This God, refuses to fall for Kama's cheap tactics; he opens his third eye and reduces Kama to ashes. But he does marry. Not a nymph, but Kamakshi, she who contains Kama in her glance.

Kamakshi is the name given to Parvati, princess of the mountains, in south India. In the east, the name given to her is Kamakhya. She holds all the symbols of Kama—the parrot, the sugarcane, the lotus flower—but while there are no temples dedicated to the god of love, Kamakshi is worshipped as a goddess.

Kamakshi's approach was radically different from Kama's. She appealed not to the base instinct of Shiva but to his higher instincts: his head and his heart. Conventional thinking says the world thrives when there is discontentment, that desire fuels market growth. But Kamakshi thought differently.

Kamakshi knew that Shiva was beyond lust. No dance would arouse him. Was there anything else besides self-gratification that would make him open his eyes? The more she thought about Shiva, the more she realized that beneath the indifference there lurked infinite compassion. She decided to tap into it.

She wanted Shiva not to reject human imperfection but to be tolerant of it. She demonstrated her intention by subjecting herself to great penance, standing on one foot and meditating, fasting, not sleeping, immersing herself for days in cold river water, and exposing herself to the elements. Eventually, sensing her integrity, shaken by her determination, Shiva came to her and agreed to do whatever she asked of him. 'Be my husband,' she said. Shiva could not say no. Kamakshi wanted him to marry not for her pleasure, nor for his either, but to save the world from destruction. Kamakshi thus got Shiva to open his eyes not in lust, but in love.

While Kama thinks of Shiva as a prey to be struck down by an arrow, Kamakshi approaches Shiva with awe and reverence. While Kama believes in instant gratification,

Kamakshi thinks of lifelong loyalty. In the Kama approach, the focus is on lust (price/incentive) rather than the bride (product/organization) or the groom (consumer/employee). In the Kamakshi approach, focus is firmly on the bride and the groom. What does the bride actually offer? Why? What does the groom seek? Why? Can there be a true wedlock, or will it be just a casual affair? This means, less discussions on trimming the cost and more discussions on consumer insights and employee feedback. This means effort, proactive activities not reactive promotions. This means actually looking at the soul of Shiva, not just his senses.

The brand manager that Chang finally selected did follow the Kamakshi approach. When asked how he would increase market share, he said, 'By making sure that our product meets the unmet need of the consumer, or by making the consumer aware of a hitherto unknown need that the product can satisfy. Our products should be able to bridge a gap in their psyche.' And when asked how he would motivate his sales force, he said, 'By appealing to their desire to be brilliant. To stoke in them the desire to conquer an impossible market.' This manager would surely work to open the eyes of Shiva.

Cynics will argue that it all comes down to money. The only reason they say that is because money is tangible and measurable, easy to understand and be turned into a graph. Passion is not. Loyalty is not. How does one capture the soul of a market on a spreadsheet? It can only be sensed. It will always remain abstract. And so, we fall into the Kama trap, reduce Maha-deva into deva, and trust the wallet, rather than have faith in the head and heart, like Kamakshi.

Yes, everyone wants a good deal. But deep down, more than a good deal, we really want to feel good about ourselves. We don't want to be seduced by discounts and incentives. We want our purchases and our employment to bring forth our glory.

33

Both sides of the fence

Once upon a time there was a young warrior who wanted to participate in the battle of Kurukshetra between the Pandavas and the Kauravas. He came to the battlefield armed with three arrows. On the way the youth met Krishna, and Krishna asked him why he was carrying only three arrows. 'With one,' he said, 'I can destroy the Pandavas, with another the Kauravas, with the third, I can kill Krishna.' Krishna asked the youth to prove it.

The youth pointed to a tree and said, 'With one arrow I can pierce each and every leaf from the tree.' Krishna asked the youth to demonstrate his skill, secretly plucking five leaves from the tree and placing it under his foot. The warrior shot an arrow, and such was the skill that the arrow pierced each and every leaf on that tree and then pierced Krishna's foot five times, once for each leaf. Krishna realized this warrior was indeed a great warrior and he could do what he claimed he could do.

Krishna asked the youth, 'On which side do you wish to fight.' The youth replied, 'I always fight on the side of the losers.'

The reply bothered Krishna: if the youth fought on the side of the losers and turned them into winners then he would immediately change sides and participate on the losing side, and help them become the winning side. Thus he would move from side to side and keep turning the losing side to winning and winning side into the losing side, creating a vicious closed loop, and a never-ending, meaningless, directionless battle.

Krishna could not allow this. He decided to destroy the warrior before he could participate in the battle. He asked the warrior, 'Will you save me from the man who plans to destroy the dharma I hope to establish on earth?' 'Sure,' said the youth, 'Point out that man and I will cut his head off.' Krishna then showed the man a mirror. 'This is he,' said Krishna. Looking at his reflection, the youth realized that Krishna wanted him dead because he felt he threatened the outcome of the battle at Kurukshetra.

'Here, take my head,' said the youth, severing his neck. Pleased with the offering, Krishna gave the youth a boon. 'Allow me to see the battle even though I am dead,' said the youth. So Krishna placed the head of the youth on a tree atop a hill and blessed the head with life so that the youth could see all the events that took place on the battlefield of Kurukshetra.

This story draws our attention to the idea of taking a stand. Krishna destroyed the warrior because he did not take a stand. He was fighting neither for the Pandavas nor for the Kauravas, neither for the right side nor the wrong side. He simply wanted to use his power to fight for the losers with the intention of making them winners, not realizing that this behaviour would lead to no conclusion. The youth was focused more on his skills and less on the outcome he desired to achieve using his skills.

Ravikishore Singh encountered a warrior such as this in his board meeting. He noticed that his most promising director spoke a lot, but never really took a stand. He would keep arguing both sides with such brilliance that it was difficult to take a call. When deliberating whether to partner with a multinational company to import a new chemical to India, the director argued eloquently on the benefits of doing so. As soon as most of the remaining board members agreed with him, he started arguing on the dangers of doing so. This gentleman was so brilliant that he could see the positive and the negative side of both the situations. And because he could see both positive and negative situations he could never take a call, nor help others take a call.

Ravikishore Singh realized the director was not really adding value—yes, he threw light on many things, but ultimately proceedings were suspended as everyone was confused. Everyone was so locked in thought that there was no action. There was, what is popularly called, paralysis by analysis. Like Krishna, Ravikishore Singh decided to stop the young director from participating in more meetings. Without him, the board could move forward, in some direction, hopefully the profitable one.

In meetings there are a lot of warriors who can play the Devil's advocate and give the opposite point of view with great clarity. But by doing so, they can sometimes block the leader from taking a decision, and moving in a particular direction. Devil's advocates are good so long as they enable the decision-making process. A good leader must be constantly aware of this. Rather than a contrarian who opposes the leader for the sake of opposition, one needs someone with a point of view, which when argued and articulated well helps the leader take a call, one way or another.

34

Curse of kingship

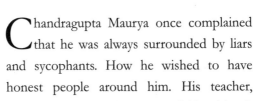

Chandragupta Maurya once complained that he was always surrounded by liars and sycophants. How he wished to have honest people around him. His teacher, Chanakya, laughed and said, 'It's the curse of kingship. A king has a sword in his hand and everyone who stands around him is acutely aware of the sword. No one knows how it will swing? So to save themselves they end up lying and flattering the king. It is fear of a king's moods and opinions that shapes the behaviour in court. Yes, you hate the liars and the sycophants, but who created them? You, only you, by simply being the king.'

Thomas, an investment banker, was preparing for his presentation late into the night. His wife asked, 'Why are you worried? Are things looking up or down?' Thomas replied, 'The market is looking up and the company has nothing to

169

worry about. I am worried about how to present it to my boss so that he does not think less of me. He is constantly judging me. If you present a growth rate more than what he feels, he will mark you as a dreamer. If you present a growth rate that is less than what he feels, he will mark you as unimaginative. Either way one is doomed. One is always defensive in front of him. One has to always strategize what one has to say.'

That very night, Thomas's boss, Cyril, was telling his wife, 'People in front of me tell me what I want to hear. I want to hear the truth, what they actually feel about the market, their jobs, our work. But it never happens.' Cyril is not even realizing that he is influencing the scene before him. He is, inadvertently, the puppet master. He is the observer creating the observation.

In an apparently logical and rational world, we forget how the behaviour of people in power influences the behaviour of people reporting to them. We can make grand statements, that we allow juniors to dissent but the juniors know that dissent rarely makes them popular. It takes a rare breed of people to be able to separate the issue from the person. Often the critic is a marked man. The marks appear in the appraisal.

It is the king who created the yes-man in court; it is the boss who created the yes-man in the corporate world. We look down upon the yes-man—but his actions stem from fear. He is afraid that if he actually says the truth, his head will be chopped off. So he tailors his dialogue such that it pleases the boss.

A good leader has to be sensitive to the power he holds over his followers. How they reflect his behaviour? How he is in a way responsible for the way they behave? If they agree with him all the time, it is more often than not an indicator that he does not like dissent. If they disagree with him all the time, it does not mean that they actually disagree with him; it can be that they have found he appreciates disagreement and so by disagreeing with them they are simply trying to win his approval. He has to be able to create an atmosphere where the issue is being addressed and it is not the boss who is being managed.

Perhaps that is the reason one often hears legends of Akbar and Birbal venturing out secretly in the city dressed as commoners to find out what is really happening; the Mughal emperor clearly did not trust official reports. He knew they were influenced by fear of the king's sword. Even the gods often approach devotees in disguise. In the *Maa Santoshi Vrat Katha*, the goddess takes the form of an ugly, old, diseased woman to check if the piety shown by her devotees is genuine or not. Even the gods know that the expressions and declarations made in the temple are not to be trusted.

35

Silent whispers

The arrival of a sage called Narada in Hindu mythology always spells trouble. He would share very innocent information, or ask a very simple question, and provoke all kinds of base emotions from jealousy to rage to insecurity.

Once he went to the house of Kansa, dictator of Mathura, who knew that the eighth son of his sister would be his killer. Kansa would have killed his sister had his brother-in-law, Vasudev, not promised to hand over the eighth child to Kansa. 'Do you trust Vasudev?' asked Narada, 'I mean, he may hand over another child and claim he is the eighth; or he may hand over his own child, say the seventh, and claim he is the eighth.' Having sowed the seeds of doubt, Narada walked away plucking his lute and chanting, 'Narayana, Narayana.' Influenced by these words, Kansa killed each and every child his sister bore to ensure his safety.

Another time, Narada went to the house of the five Pandava brothers who had a common wife called Draupadi, and told them the story of a nymph called Tilottama. 'Two demon brothers, Sunda and Upasunda, fell in love with her and wanted to marry her. She said she would marry the stronger of the two. So the two brothers fought to prove their strength. Since both were equally matched, they killed each other. Wonder which of you five is the strongest?' Hearing this the five Pandava brothers quickly put down rules that would govern the sharing of a wife; she would be with one brother exclusively for a year and return to him after spending four years with the other four brothers.

In Kansa's case, Narada's intervention leads to serial infanticide. In the Pandavas' case, Narada's intervention secures domestic bliss. Yet, at no point is Narada feared or shunned by any king or god. In fact his arrival is welcomed. His intervention is seen as something inherently good—though the goodness is not immediately apparent. In Kansa's case, Kansa sees him as a well-wisher. But by his intervention, Narada ensures that Vasudev, rather than handing over the prophesized eighth child as he initially planned to, takes the child to a safe house where he can grow up and return to kill the wicked king.

Narada, though a mischief-maker and quarrel-monger, has the well-being of people at heart.

But there are advisers whose intentions are otherwise. The most famous one of these is Manthara who poisons the ear of Kaikeyi, in the epic Ramayana, and influences the queen to

Leader: 50 Insights from Mythology

demand the exile of Rama. By following Manthara's advice, Kaikeyi destroys the household.

So who is the advisor who sits beside the king: Narada or Manthara? If Narada, how does he see the king—as Kansa or as a Pandava? These are difficult questions for a leader to answer. For the Naradas of today's world do not come with a lute and Mantharas of today's world are not bent and ugly.

Jagruti is amongst the first women in her company to become the unit head of an entire zone. It is a powerful and enviable position and she knows that there are many people who would like her to fail. As she took over office, she found many people willing to be her friend and confidant. There is Nitin, an accountant who has worked in the zone for over twenty years. A mild-mannered man, Nitin tells her what is happening in every office in the zone. So does Suresh, the administration manager, who has been in the organization for six years and is clearly very ambitious. Often the data they give her and the opinions they voice are similar. But sometimes they are diametrically different. And she wonders who the Narada is and who the Manthara.

One can argue that Jagruti should encourage neither Nitin nor Suresh. But when one is made responsible for a zone for ₹50 crores with 200 employees and is expected to show results in six months, one has no choice but to rely on the views and opinions of people who have been around and who can ramp up her learning curve. Data in excel sheets are not enough. Yes, Jagruti will eventually meet all her 200 subordinates and make up her own mind but in the meanwhile she needs some information about the motivations and personality styles of her regional and area managers and her vendors and even her team.

Jagruti is acutely aware that being a woman, most men are wary of her and do not know how to relate to a woman in a position of power. She wonders sometimes if Nitin or Suresh are being patronizing. She wonders if they are manipulating her, making her take decisions to serve their own ends. She wonders if they have her best interests in mind. Maybe they are working for people higher up in the organization who want her to fail. Suspicion fills her mind often. And so does faith. Maybe they are genuinely good people. Who knows? In real life, no one comes with haloes or horns. Distinguishing Narada from Manthara is not easy. Whether their advice is for the good of the organization or for their own self-interests will be realized only in hindsight.

36

Implied needs

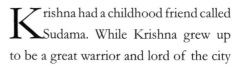Krishna had a childhood friend called Sudama. While Krishna grew up to be a great warrior and lord of the city of Dwaraka, Sudama remained a poor priest. Desperate for some wealth, Sudama paid Krishna a visit in Dwaraka. But on reaching there he felt too embarrassed to ask for anything. He simply gave his friend a packet of puffed rice, which was all he could afford, and claimed he just wanted to see his old friend. Krishna sensed his friend's need and very silently ensured that when Sudama returned home he found his house overflowing with wealth, much to his delight and surprise

The same Krishna had another friend called Arjuna, who had to fight a great war against his cousins. Just before the fight, he lost his nerves. The thought of killing his own relatives, however justified, horrified him. He did not know what to do. It was here that Krishna sang the song now known as the

Bhagavad Gita. The words of the song addressed Arjuna's core issues, cleared his mind, clarified his doubts, enabled him to raise his bow and fight the enemy with conviction.

Neither Sudama nor Arjuna was explicit about what they wanted. But Krishna sensed what they needed. This sensitivity is something leaders must possess. A retired army colonel joined a cosmetics company as their administration manager. All his life he lived a cushioned life in the army, not realizing the expense of some of the perks he received; so when he joined civilian life he was quite satisfied with the salary he was offered by the company until he had to pay for some of the things he took for granted in the army. He realized his salary was not enough to support his lifestyle. He also realized that had he been aware of these expenses he could have negotiated a more appropriate salary. But he had missed the boat. Too proud to ask for more, he kept quiet. The owner of the cosmetics company, however, sensed something was amiss. He noticed that the colonel took the company bus instead of his car several times a week. A few inquiries and he figured out what was happening. Very discreetly, the finance department was told to make changes in the colonel's salary structure. A smile returned on the Colonel's face. Just like Sudama's.

More importantly, Krishna knew what to give to whom—wealth to Sudama and wisdom to Arjuna. Imagine what would have happened if he sang the Bhagavad Gita to Sudama! Or gave wealth to Arjuna! When people enter a leader's room, they come expecting to receive something. And leaders have to be sensitive enough to figure out what exactly they are seeking and respond accordingly. It is not always what they are asking!

When Mukul entered his CEO's room to check if the presentation to be made before the board was in order, the CEO, Rajnikant, went through the presentation and said, it was okay. Mukul left the room unsatisfied. He knew it was in order, but he wanted something else from his boss, a few words of validation and even, praise, to soothe his nerves. He was terrified of the presentation. He feared that if things went wrong his reputation would be ruined. He wanted Rajnikant to comfort him, but was too embarrassed to state it. He wanted to know if Rajnikant would support him if things went wrong. He wanted the feeling of support, not a curt 'it is okay'.

Sensitivity to what people want is not something that can be taught in business schools. It has to be developed. It is an implicit expectation from leaders. Rajnikant expects everyone to state their needs in a checklist, preferably an Excel sheet. Modern businesses often talk about transparency and stating what one needs very clearly. But humans are usually not transparent. It is embarrassing for people to openly admit that they have financial issues. It is awkward, even beneath one's dignity, for a senior director to admit that he is nervous. What is apparent is usually not the truth. What a leader needs to focus on is what lies beneath the apparent.

37

They don't have to think like you

In the Ramayana, Hanuman, the monkey god, is known as the greatest devotee of Rama. It was he who had located Rama's wife, Sita, in Lanka, after she had been abducted by the rakshasa king, Ravana.

The story goes that, after the discovery of Sita's whereabouts, Hanuman had, of his own volition, set aflame the city of Lanka. This had displeased Rama as he had no desire to hurt the residents of Lanka for the crime of their king. Not wanting to displease Rama ever again, Hanuman swore never to take any decision without consulting with Rama.

This absolute obedience became so intense that it alarmed Jambuvan, the wise bear, who also served in the army of animals raised by Rama to defeat Ravana and liberate Sita. When Hanuman was being given instructions of where he would find the Sanjivani herb that could save Rama's brother, Laxman, from certain death after being injured in battle, Jambuvan told Rama, 'Make sure to clearly tell him to come back with the herb after he finds it. Otherwise, he will find the herb and simply wait by the mountain, in complete compliance.' This was not good, Rama realized. The situation had to be rectified.

And so it came to pass, as retold in the *Adbhut Ramayana*, during the course of the war, Ravana's cousin, Mahiravan, a sorcerer, managed to abduct both Rama and Laxman, and take them to Patala, his subterranean kingdom. Only Hanuman had the intellectual and physical prowess to rescue them. He had to rely on his own wits; there was no Rama around to instruct him. He was on his own. Jambuvan realized this situation was of Rama's own making; Hanuman was being forced to rise up to the challenge.

At one point of the rescue mission, Hanuman had to simultaneously blow out five lamps located in five corners of Patala. He solved this problem by sprouting four extra heads: that of a boar, an eagle, a lion and a horse. With five heads he could blow out five lamps located in five directions easily. Eventually, Hanuman succeeded in rescuing Rama. He had transformed from an obedient servant to an astute independent decision-maker. He had transformed from Rama-bhakt to Mahavir, from god (in lower case) to God (capitalized), worthy of veneration in his own right. Rama had thus created a leader.

A time comes in every leader's life when he has to create leaders around him. This involves making people around him competent enough to take independent decisions. But this is not easy. Every decision has consequences, not all of them acceptable to a leader. It demands tremendous restraint and maturity on a leader's part not to intervene and change the decision made by a junior.

Hanuman's decision of burning Lanka displeased Rama. And so after that, Hanuman stopped taking decisions. To rectify the damage done, Rama had to remove himself from the scene so that Hanuman could rediscover his decision-making abilities. A leader need not agree with a junior's decision. They are two different people and so may not see the same situation in the same way. But to imagine that the junior will think just like them, is many a leader's folly. Sanjeev is one such leader.

Sanjeev's brilliant decision-making abilities have resulted in his becoming a partner in a consulting firm at a very early age. Now he has to nurture his managers and nudge them to take more responsibilities. One manager, Sebastian, on his own, decided to follow up on the status of a business proposal with a client. 'Why did you do that?' shouted Sanjeev, 'It can put them off.' Another time, Sebastian gave a half-day off to a management trainee who was feeling unwell. 'Why did you do that?' screamed Sanjeev, 'There is so much work to do.' After this, not wanting to upset his boss further, Sebastian stopped taking any decisions. He just did what Sanjeev told him to do. During appraisals, Sanjeev said, 'You need to be more proactive,' to Sebastian's astonishment and great irritation.

Sanjeev wants Sebastian to be proactive but any signs of

proactive behaviour is immediately reprimanded. As a result, Sanjeev is surrounded by obedient followers and no leaders. Sanjeev does not trust his managers unless they think exactly like him, which is impossible. Potential leaders, unable to handle Sanjeev's demand for proactive behaviour followed by reprimand of all independent decisions, have left the organization. Sebastian is planning to leave too. And he will, until Sanjeev realizes that to groom leaders he has to allow them to take decisions and stand by them, no matter what. This indicates trust. Only in trust does growth happen.

38

Packaging matters

The sage Uttanka stood in the middle of the desert. He was suddenly thirsty. He remembered a promise made to him by Krishna long ago, 'I will bring you the nectar of the gods whenever you genuinely yearn for it.' Yes, that is what Uttanka genuinely wanted at that moment: nectar of the gods. He shut his eyes and wished for it. He opened his eyes, expecting a smiling Krishna to stand there with a cup brimming with sparkling nectar. There was no Krishna. There was no one, just a vast sandy emptiness stretching to the horizon.

Uttanka was irritated. He shut his eyes once more and wished for nectar and remembered Krishna fervently. This time when he opened his eyes, he saw a beggar covered with filth holding a dirty stinking bowl in his hand. It contained water. 'Drink,' said the beggar, 'You look thirsty.' Uttanka turned away from him, repelled by his ugliness. The beggar went away.

Uttanka was now parched. In fury he yelled, 'Keep your promise, Krishna.' A voice boomed from the sky, 'I did. I forced Indra to offer you a bowl of nectar. He just did. And you just refused.' It dawned on Uttanka that the filthy beggar who offered him a bowl of water was actually Indra offering him nectar. He had assumed how Indra should look. He had paid a price for his assumption.

There are many Uttankas in the corporate world, men who believe packaging is an indicator of content. Prashant is one such Uttanka. He is the owner of a medium-sized BPO. One of his young executives, Suhas, came up with a wonderful idea of shift rotation to improve performance and reduce attrition. Suhas was a young man of twenty-six who had spent five years in the BPO learning the ropes. He did not know English but that did not matter since the calls he serviced were for the local market. He was not even a graduate; he could not afford to go to college and needed to work. He was hired by the organization because he came very cheap. But despite his background, Suhas was extremely sharp and sensitive. He recognized the problem that the BPO was facing and came up with a deceptively simple way of overcoming it.

Unfortunately, when Suhas presented the solution to Prashant, he found himself being dismissed. Prashant did not even hear him out completely because he assumed someone as young, poor and barely qualified as Suhas could not possibly solve his problems. A year later, Prashant hired a consultant.

After six months of investigation, the solution that emerged was exactly what Suhas had come up with almost eighteen months earlier. Prashant kicked himself for not listening to Suhas as he signed the cheque for his very expensive consultant.

Sandeep, however, has accepted the existence of Uttankas in the marketplace. He has to deal with many governmental agencies. He knows that whenever he asks for an appointment, he will not get it. He will be shunted from one desk to another. Ministers and bureaucrats simply give him the runaround. In frustration, he came up with a rather shallow idea. He hired Bob, a tall blonde big-built bearded Australian youth, who was keen to gain some experience in third-world markets. Bob was given the designation of chief consumer strategist. Every time Bob called the government agencies, he was given appointments. Sandeep knew it was because of his Australian drawl. Every time Bob entered the offices, along with Sandeep, he was taken straight to the minister or the senior bureaucrats, the very same people who never gave Sandeep the time of the day.

In wry amusement, Sandeep observed how everyone ignored the fact that Bob was too young to be a chief anything. Bob gave a small speech after which Sandeep made the real pitch. Invariably, the deal would go through. Sandeep was very happy. One day, he told Bob, 'They are so eager to impress the white guy that they are willing to sign on any paper. That makes you a very useful tool for my business.' Bob did not feel bad at the racist jibe; he was learning an important lesson in marketing. For some people what matters more is the packaging, even at the cost of the content.

39

Challenging loyalty

Ramayana speaks of two brothers, Vibhishana and Kumbhakarna. Vibhishana refuses to support his elder brother Ravana who abducts the wife of Rama. Kumbhakarna, however, stands by his brother, even though he does not agree with Ravana's actions. Vibhishana is a disloyal defector while Kumbhakarna is a loyal brother. The scriptures celebrate Vibhishana. While every year, during festivals, the effigy of Kumbhakarna is burnt alongside his brother.

In the Mahabharata, Karna owes his meteoric rise in station, from the son of a charioteer to warlord and king, to Duryodhana, who refuses to return the land of the Pandavas. Karna stays loyal to Duryodhana till the very end, refusing the most tempting bribes offered by Krishna. For this he is ruthlessly killed under instructions of Krishna.

The scriptures challenge the traditional notion of loyalty. Loyalty is not seen as an end in itself. It is seen merely as a means. If the end is not noble (as in the case of Karna and Kumbhakarna) it is not venerated.

In the modern corporate world, what matters more: talent or loyalty? What affects the balance sheet?

During the annual appraisals, Madhukar was furious. He had received the same bonus as Champaklal. But he had done so much more work. He had turned around a loss-making unit into a profitable one in less than a year. He had cut costs and acquired new customers. Thanks to him, the company was on an accelerated growth curve. In comparison, Champaklal had done nothing but sustain running a marginally profitable unit. That unit had so much potential that Champaklal refused to tap. Why couldn't the owner of the company see that?

But the owner of the company saw things differently. He told the CFO as they were finalizing the bonus, 'Madhukar is an MBA, a professional. Sooner or later, he will leave us and go to another company where he will be paid more. We will never be able to match up the competition. Champaklal will never leave us. He may not be a great stallion but he is a dependable donkey. Horses will come and go, adding bursts of success, but donkeys grant us sustainable slow growth. We must reward both equally.'

In the uncertain world of business, loyalty offers comfort to owners. This is an emotional need whose value is not understood by professionals. Champaklal will never be as smart as Madhukar but he is able to satisfy an emotional need

Leader: 50 Insights from Mythology

of the owner. Madhukar's brilliance makes the owner insecure. Retaining talent is not easy. In Madhukar's case, the owner has to make active efforts to retain him. In Champaklal's case, the owner is passive; he knows that Champaklal's mediocre talents ensure he will never look out for another opportunity. Champaklal's low returns are compensated by the high assurance he offers. And this matters in the owner's strategic long-term balance sheet.

The owner sees Madhukar as Vibhishan and Champaklal as Kumbhakarna. Some of the practices that the owner follows are not quite ethical. He knows that Madhukar will shy away from these practices or at least demand a hefty pound of flesh in exchange. Champaklal, aware of his low market value, will do the unethical tasks quietly and will ask for no extra reward. Champaklal may not be as talented, but like Karna he will not be tempted by any Krishna and like Karna he will be ready to die in the battlefield. For this he needs to be rewarded.

40

Children of the blind

In the epic Mahabharata, Duryodhana, the eldest Kaurava, is the villain. His envy results in a great war where millions are killed. He cannot bear the success of his cousins, the Pandavas. He wants them to be destroyed. He wants them to suffer and die. He refuses to part with even a needle-tip of land for his cousins for the sake of peace. He destroys his own peace of mind and the well-being of his household so as to destroy his enemies. Such hatred! Where does it come from?

What creates a Duryodhana? A man so bitter and angry that he refuses to focus on his own good fortune (good parents, good wife, good friend, good inheritance) and focuses instead on the fortune of his cousins, and gets miserable by constantly comparing. His whole life is spent comparing and feeling inadequate and unhappy.

Vyasa, author of the epic, without being explicit about it,

points to the possible origin of his personality. Duryodhana's father, Dhritarashtra, is blind. His mother, Gandhari, is blindfolded. The father cannot see the son. The mother refuses to see her son (whatever her reason). So a son grows up unseen by his parents. No one notices the child's growing sense of inadequacy, no one notices the child, growing up full of rage. No one therefore corrects him. The child succumbs to flattery. The child is indulged and the result is disastrous.

Organizations are full of Duryodhanas, employees with a sense of inadequacy and rage that reflects in their decision-making abilities. More than achieving organizational goals, they want to impose their personalities every time a decision is made. For example, they fight more for the larger cabin and a larger team and a larger compensation than for the business. The gaze is more towards themselves than towards the customer. They are constantly screaming for attention. But the one who has to give it to them—the management—is often either blind or blindfolded. They either cannot see him or they don't want to see him.

Ramesh is a Duryodhana. He believes he is the best sales manager in his company. He has brought in more qualitative and quantitative growth than any other sales manager in his company. But he feels, his managing director does not see him. The MD treats all sales managers equally, giving them equal bonuses and equal attention. The MD has no favourites. Ramesh wants attention. He wants to be loved and acknowledged. The MD does not even notice this need; he assumes everyone in his team is, or at least should be, professional. Emotional needs are something that he does not notice, or he refuses to notice. As a result of his extreme professionalism, he has become Gandhari. Some would say, he is a Dhritarashtra, he is incapable of being sensitive to his team. The result is that all his sales managers, Ramesh included, feel like children of a blind parent. Their desire for attention manifests in all kinds of behaviours—fights in the boardroom, lack of team work, refusal to cooperate, demands for more time with the MD (which he refuses to give), demand for more perks and rewards and recognition, beyond what is officially allowed (which is not forthcoming).

The organization is facing the brunt of Ramesh's rage and sense of inadequacy. Everyone is wondering why Ramesh cannot be more professional, do his job and go home. They forget that Ramesh is not a machine. He has emotional needs. He wants to be seen and acknowledged and appreciated. This need of his may be argued as irrational and stupid, but it remains his need, nevertheless. In imagination, humans may be capable of cutting out their emotions every time they enter the office, but it does not happen in reality. Organizations may see humans as cogs in a wheel, but this mechanistic view is theoretical, not practical. Every human being has emotional needs that need pampering, howsoever silly it may seem.

The MD needs to realize this role in the turmoil that is faced by the organization. Gandhari and Dhritarashtra are as much responsible for the Mahabharata war as Duryodhana.

41

The weak in the pack

I am the CEO of a multinational company. My company has a policy of weeding off the bottom 10 per cent of performers. I don't agree with the policy because the appraisal process of the company is not robust enough to capture a true and fair picture of the contribution of employees. Do you agree that for a company to have a solid employee base, it's necessary to fire people every year?

 There is no right way to do business and there is no wrong. There are only actions and consequences. This is the very Indian approach to do business. A Western approach seeks to do the right thing, and in doing so they rationalize some of the most cruel of practices, such as weeding out the bottom 10 per cent of performers.

Appraisal processes notwithstanding, let us appreciate what is actually happening over here. The organization imagines itself as a pack of predators out to hunt. To ensure you are 'lean and mean', you need to rid yourself of laggards who hold you back. You need the strongest in your team. By that logic, this approach makes sense.

This action also instills fear in the pack, a fear that you could be the next one to be fired. Fear is a powerful motivator. We work harder in fear. We are always on our toes.

The pack of predators exists to capture Lakshmi, goddess of wealth, from the marketplace. Those who are unable to capture Lakshmi or contribute to the capture of Lakshmi are seen as losers or not fit for the pack. They have to be discarded.

Fundamentally, we have to ask why the organization exists. Is it a pride of lionesses that exists to hunt prey, so that the lion (shareholders) may feast on it? If yes, the weak will be kicked out. This approach visualizes the market as a jungle full of rival competitors and prey who can outrun the predator. This is rana-bhoomi, the battleground where there is no room for weakness. Here, the organization has to survive and so is willing to get rid of its weak link.

But we can see the organization as an ecosystem that helps people grow and thrive, a place where the strong help the weak rather than rejecting them. Where appraisals are a way to figure out what more needs to be done to enable even the weakest member of the pack to hunt. Here the organization turns into ranga-bhoomi, a nurturing playground, an ecosystem that you enter in order to grow. But the risk is that people can turn complacent here, take advantage of the kindness of the leader and not be paranoid about succeeding. Some may even dismiss this idea as utopian. For the cynic, battlegrounds are truth; playgrounds are fantasy.

When the battle is announced, Ravana kicks out those who do not fall in line with his appraisal (Vibhishana) and wakes up those who sleep (Kumbhakarna). Ravana is a great king who grabs and captures Lakshmi. But in the Indian way, he is unworthy of worship, for the purpose of an organization and the role of a leader is about outgrowing fear, not amplifying it.

42

Law-abiding professionals

Rama of the Ramayana is known as maryada purushottama, the one who upholds the law under any circumstances. He is what we would call 100 per cent compliant in the corporate world. This makes Rama worthy of worship. But the scriptures are not naive. They do not believe that obedience and compliance make for a better world.

Rama's compliance for the law is a good thing at the start of the epic Ramayana when he obeys the decree of his father who is also the king, and forsakes all right to the throne. But later in the epic, when he orders that his wife, the innocent Sita be taken out of Ayodhya simply because the law states a queen's reputation should never be the subject of malicious gossip, we wonder if upholding law is such a good thing.

It is in the Mahabharata, where the whole concept of

upholding the law is made topsy-turvy. Duryodhana, the villain of the epic, upholds the law at all times. He never breaks it. His uncle, Shakuni, breaks it; but never he. He broke no law when he invited his cousins, the Pandavas, to the game of dice; he broke no law when the Pandavas wagered their wife Draupadi; he broke no law when he ordered her disrobing as by law, one can do anything one wants with a slave! Thus by upholding the law, one can also be a villain.

Both Rama and Duryodhana abide by the law, keep the rules, follow the processes 100 per cent but only one is worthy of worship. The other is equated with a demon. Why? Because there is something that we cannot see—their motivation. Because in the scriptures, Rama is identified as Vishnu; we know his motivation is the welfare of the world. Duryodhana, however, is motivated by his own welfare at the cost of every living creature. Rama follows the rule for the benefit of the organization. Duryodhana follows the rule for his own benefit. Rama is 100 per cent compliant so that the company can achieve its target. Duryodhana is 100 per cent mimic so that he gets his bonus. Rama believes in what he does. Duryodhana does not believe in what he is doing; he simply agrees to disagree, aligns as a good team player, and plays along because he is a professional!

The institutional model of management is based on processes and process compliance, and we consider that a good thing. In an industrial economy where workers were simply expected to finish a set of tasks and the tasks had no emotional or intellectual component, this worked well. But in a knowledge economy where intellectual and emotional contribution is critical, enforcing compliance is not easy.

Vivek wants to make sure that he gets 100 per cent of the promised bonus. For that he has to get 5 out of 5 on appraisal, something that according to the 'bell curve' of the company, less than 10 per cent of the employees can get. So he has spent the past three months doing everything that the boss has asked him to do. He knows that obeying his boss and ensuring that the boss feels like a boss guarantee him that score. He does his tasks exactly the way the boss tells him to, he makes fun of all the people the boss makes fun of, he admires everyone the boss admires, he reads the same books his boss reads, he does everything to please his boss. In his team, there are people who are much better at work, and who are of greater value strategically for the organization. But they do not invest as much time on the boss. And so while Vivek and others get a equal score on quantitative matters, only Vivek gets full score on qualitative matters. A week after Vivek got his bonus and his raise, he submitted his resignation and moved on to the next job and to the next boss. And the boss, who had told the management how committed and deserving Vivek was, felt like a fool. A victim of yet another corporate Duryodhana.

43

Rejection of the rest

In the Mahabharata, after the city of Indraprastha is built, Yudhishthira was crowned king in the presence of all the kings of the earth. Following the coronation, the priests asked him to honour his guests. But the first to be honoured should be the one whom they respected the most. Yudhishthira and his brothers, the Pandavas, were unanimous in their choice of who should be honoured first—Krishna, friend, philosopher and guide. And so Krishna was made to sit in a special seat and his feet were washed and he was garlanded and offered gifts. Thus the Pandavas expressed their gratitude. Unfortunately, the other guests took this as an insult. In paying Krishna attention, they had neglected the others. They were angry that the Pandavas chose a man who was not even king, and who was raised by cowherds, as the chief guest. They felt insulted. Surely, one amongst them was more worthy. The kings raised objections, tempers flared, angry words were exchanged and finally violence broke out, resulting in a messy end to a great event.

Decisions do not exist in isolation. They are perceived differently by different people. Each one perceives it from his or her own point of view. Thus every decision contributes to the measure of one's own value. And this can be very tricky. For what may be seen as good by one can be seen as terrible by many, a personal affront even if that is not the issue.

As the stock market collapsed, Biswajeet became very insecure. As CEO, his reputation was at stake. He had worked very hard with his team to improve the market capitalization of his small company and now this, for no fault of his, due to some strange event in Europe. Not knowing what to do, he wandered the office corridors when he met Jayant, his young and competent general manager. They had started their career together but Biswajeet had moved ahead because he clearly had the brains. Jayant had remained a good friend. 'Come, have coffee with me,' he said and took Jayant to his cabin. They spent an hour talking about their early years, being nostalgic, anything to forget the horror of the falling share prices. Biswajeet just wanted to calm down and feel normal. But his sitting with Jayant for an hour got the rumour mills working across the maze of office corridors. The CFO got annoyed: surely, he was the confidant in such situations. The COO got irritated: was this a suggestion that Jayant was being considered as his replacement? The company secretary was angry: why was so much time being given to Jayant by the otherwise busy CEO? Biswajeet's team imagined all kinds of reasons for his meeting with Jayant. They felt he was signalling that they did not matter to him anymore as they had failed to achieve the desired objective. Everyone saw it from their point of view, not from his point of view. Their rage and their anger was a manifestation of their own insecurity and their doubts on the relationship they shared with Biswajeet. A tiny event triggered a crisis.

44

Masculine and feminine leaders

 We are conditioned to associate emotions with gender. So toughness is associated with masculinity, tenderness with femininity; domination with masculinity and submissiveness with femininity; rationality with masculinity and creativity with femininity; intelligence with masculinity and intuition with femininity; penetration with masculinity and receptivity with femininity; power with masculinity and love with femininity; straightforwardness is associated with masculinity and manipulation with femininity. Leaders are asked to get in touch with their masculine and feminine sides, whatever that means.

The male brain and the female brain are really not structurally different but one is drenched in testosterone and the other is drenched in oestrogen and so there are bound to be differences in how men and women react to crises. Upbringing and education contributes to differences.

Some emotions may be more associated with men and women in statistical terms, but this changes dramatically with age, exposure and culture. In Hindu mythologies, when Rama is compared with Krishna, we are told Rama is more masculine and Krishna more feminine (Krishna even plaits his hair and sports a nose ring in many artworks). But both Rama and Krishna are forms of Vishnu who is clearly more feminine than the very masculine Shiva.

Yet in local legends near Mathura, Shiva takes the form of a milkmaid to dance with Krishna who is the complete man (purna purush) and so becomes adored as Gopeshwar. And in the local legends of Tamil Nadu, Shiva takes the form of a midwife to deliver the child of a female devotee. Like Vishnu who often turns into Mohini and does not take the help of nymphs, Shiva chooses not to take the help of his wife, Gauri.

Amongst goddesses, we are told the demure Gauri is more feminine than Durga, who marches into battle with weapons, but Kali, the wild one who drinks blood, remains a feminist icon. The silent Sita is seen as more feminine than the demanding, vengeful Draupadi.

Somehow, mythology does not align well to the standard clichéd gender divides, at least not Hindu mythology. In Western mythology, God is decidedly masculine. The goddess, once a key feature of all mythologies, is all but wiped out. She is at best mother, daughter, sister or wife. In Hindu mythology, she is all that and more. The problem is that we look at images of male and female deities and assume that the relationship between them reflects gender politics of society. Perhaps it is time to relook at this assumption.

In the Puranas, the male form is used to indicate the mind and the female form is used to indicate the world that the mind perceives. Thus gender-neutral ideas are represented through gendered forms. It is likely that someone will ask: why is woman not the mind? Here the assumption is that mind is superior to the world around us, and so Puranas reiterate gender hierarchy. But the reason is rather different. In Indian metaphysics, mind (inner world) and society (outer world) have an uneasy relationship, each one claiming to be superior to the other in different schools.

Thus in Vedanta, society is maya (delusion) and the mind is Shiva (pure, untainted by delusion) while in tantra, society is shakti (power) that animates the corpse-like mind (shava) into being Shiva. The reason the mind is seen as masculine and society feminine is that just as ideas of the mind can only be given a 'form' externally in the world, the reproductive power of a man can only be realized through the body of a woman.

The male form thus lends itself best to represent the mind and the female form for matter. So the male forms represent the entrepreneur (male or female) and the female forms represent the enterprise (neuter). As is the entrepreneur, so is the enterprise. If the entrepreneur is like Shiva, indifferent, the enterprise turns into Kali, wild and so demanding attention.

When the entrepreneur is Shankara, paying attention, the enterprise calms down as Gauri. If the entrepreneur is like Rama, the follower of rules, the enterprise can be like Sita, silent and obedient, or like Surpanakha, who will demand attention and who will not be violently forced into submission.

If the entrepreneur is Krishna, the enterprise will be dynamic, sometimes like Satyabhama, who demands love, and sometimes like Rukmini, who gives love, and sometimes like Radha and Draupadi, who though belonging to another, draw attention and care. As is God, so is Goddess. As is team leader, so is the team. As is entrepreneur, so is the enterprise. In the absence of God (the human mind), there is no enterprise. The Goddess then is nature (independent of human control). She does not need him but he certainly needs her.

45

Competitors and collaborators

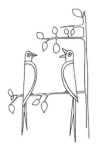

In a pack of wolves we find collaboration and competition. The wolves collaborate to hunt a deer. After the hunt is complete they compete for the flesh, with the alpha taking the biggest bite. In a herd of deer also we find collaboration and competition. The deer collaborate to protect the young from predators. But they compete as to who is at the front of the herd (safest spot) and who is the laggard at the back and who is in the flanks.

Management today gives us mixed signals. What is better? To be collaborative or competitive? There is talk of how employees should collaborate with each other yet there is reward and recognition on the basis of meritocracy, which evokes intense competition between colleagues. Why would I collaborate with someone who will eventually take the credit as team leader and become my boss?

In the Ramayana, Rama does not compete with his brothers and gives up all claims to the kingdom, something that is mirrored by his half-brother Bharata too. Ravana, on the other hand, competes with his brother Kubera, eventually drives him out of Lanka and lays claim to the city.

In the Mahabharata, the Pandavas collaborate with each other, sharing kingdom and wife, and standing up against the Kauravas. They are unable to collaborate with the Kauravas. And there is a hint of resentment at being forced to collaborate with each other, for Arjuna gets only 20 per cent of the wife he wins as trophy in an archery contest. No one asks Draupadi, wife of the five Pandavas, what she wants. Whether she wants the winner of the competition (Arjuna) or the participants of the collaboration (the Pandavas). Competition between the Pandavas and the Kauravas results in her public humiliation. Collaboration amongst the Pandavas enables her to avenge that humiliation.

Both competition and collaboration have their advantages. Competition helps us identify who the strongest and smartest is. Collaboration enables us to take advantage of everybody's talents.

Both competition and collaboration have disadvantages too. Competition weeds out the weak, creating an ecosystem of extreme insecurity. Collaboration gives room to the weak, creating an ecosystem of complacency amongst those with little talent and frustration amongst those with a lot of talent.

The danger we face in organizations is not recognizing both as forces, each with its place in the jungle that is the market.

We find people evangelizing collaboration over competition, or vice versa. Some project collaboration as feminine and good and competition as masculine and bad. Some project collaboration as the answer to life's problems as it is more inclusive and respects diversity. Others project collaboration as the game of sissies, a safety valve for those who cannot compete.

It all depends on context. In some markets we need competition. Here teamwork is essentially alignment to a single goal. In some markets we need collaboration. Here teamwork is about making oneself dependable to others. In the former, we are part of the solution that has already been figured out. In the latter, we are part of the team that figures out the problem and finds the solution.

In the MBA ecosystem of the corporate world, where ambitious, highly paid professionals are hired for doing top jobs, where being CEO is aspirational, it is foolish to expect collaboration. Most see themselves as alpha and want only a pack, or herd, that bows to their will. They will at best bow to whom they consider to be an alpha, and will collaborate after submission, out of deference, to please the alpha. The alpha is not indicated by the designation. It is a function of capacity and capability. If the ambitious, highly paid professional discovers that the person he reports to is not good enough, he goes out of his way to prove his incompetence (usually through non-collaboration and even subversion). In other words, he competes for the top job by proving that his boss cannot collaborate and build a team.

Management, with its obsession for processes, ignores the people who love power. Power makes them feel secure. Security can either come from being the dominant one who directs others or the submissive one who is given clear directions by the dominant one. Skills notwithstanding, not everyone has the capability to compete or collaborate. Some find competition highly addictive. Others find collaboration highly comforting. To expect people to switch from one mindset to another, at the will and whim of the management, is perhaps expecting too much.

46

The auditor's tragedy

On hearing Rama's cries of help, Sita insisted that Lakshmana go to his rescue. Lakshmana hesitated. If he went out to help Rama, who would protect Sita? He came up with a solution: He drew a line around their grass hut. 'Stay within!' he told his sister-in-law, 'Within is culture, where you are safe. Without is the forest, where no one is safe.'

This story of Lakshmana Rekha, the line drawn by Lakshmana around Sita's hut, comes to us from regional Ramayanas like the Bengali *Krittivasa Ramayana* and the Telugu *Ranganatha Ramayana,* written about seven centuries ago. It is not found in the old Sanskrit Ramayana of Valmiki, written two thousand years ago, or even the oldest regional Ramayana, written in Tamil by Kamban, a thousand years ago.

How do we view the Lakshmana Rekha? A symbol of

love, created by a young man to protect his sister-in-law? Or as a symbol of oppression, created by a man to control the movements of a woman. In the twenty-first century, much of feminist literature has conditioned us to see it as the latter. Lakshmana, at best, comes across as a patronizing patriarch. So is it in business.

Rules are created to protect organizations. Some rules create efficiency while others de-risk the company. Together they contribute to the prosperity and security of the company. Together they ensure the organization becomes controllable, predictable and manageable. Various technologies are created to ensure that people follow the rules. There are technologies to communicate the rules: the various protocols, guidelines, regulations, procedures and policies. There are technologies to measure if the rules are being followed or violated. There are technologies to flag repeat violations and escalate issues. Essentially, rules help us domesticate and organize ourselves.

Then come the auditors: the internal and external, who check if we have complied. They go through our documents and our spending patterns and check if investor wealth is safe, and if implementation aligns with the strategies and tactics agreed upon, and if the organization fulfils its obligations to society by paying taxes on time, and explaining all its costs and expenses that erode into profit. The auditor is the Lakshmana of the organization, protecting the institution for the board of directors and investors.

The analogy can upset many people for it equates Sita to the institution and makes her a property of Rama. It endorses patriarchy. Yet the relationship between the board of directors and the institution is the same as between Rama and Sita. Without the institution (Sita), the board of directors (Rama) have no value or purpose, or even meaning. Their entire existence depends on nourishing and protecting the institution, and the institution in exchange makes them valuable and glamorous, worthy of respect, even worship.

It is the auditor (Lakshmana) who ensures that the institution is safe. He ensures that rules are followed and even creates rules to ensure other rules are followed. To the people in the organization, he can seem like an oppressor. For his actions limit movement. His demands take away freedom and agility. The larger the company, the larger the investments, the more the rules, the more important the auditor, the less nimble is the organization. It takes away quick decisions, and puts obstacles on the entrepreneurial spirit.

It is the auditor who is hauled up when it turns out that the promoter has been misusing investor wealth to increase personal wealth at the cost of the institution. In other words, the one who is supposed to be Rama turns into Ravana and gets the institution to break rules for his own benefit. It is the auditor who has to prove his honesty, and diligence, when there is a takeover. We often mock the auditor, or the company secretary, as the oppressor who forces us to comply with rules we don't want to, who retards us, makes us inflexible and not very nimble, especially when we are a large organization. But he is Rama's younger brother, loyal and determined to protect all that his brother stands for.

47

Wrapped in rhythms

Modern management, immersed in Americana, loves habits. Good habits, of course. Habits are repetitive actions that we do unconsciously, on cue. We don't think much about them. We get used to doing them, and do them efficiently, and get agitated when we are unable to do them. In many ways, it is Pavlonian conditioning, a well-trained dog of a mind, that salivates automatically when the bell is rung.

In many ways, it is the opposite of what is taught in yoga and other Indian spiritual practices, which speak of awareness (dharana) and attention (dhyana), to all actions. To do things consciously, not unconsciously. To be mindful, not mindless, when we are acting. To be sensitive and caring, adapting to the context, not doing it because that is just the way we are, hard-wired to function in a particular way, going to the gym, come rain or shine, because we have made a habit of it.

In the Hindu architecture of the universe, there is a fundamental divide between mind and matter, the psychological and the physical realm. Not so in Americana, this values the material, the tangible, the measurable, much more than the intangible mercurial mind.

In fact, the Americans inherited this from the Europeans. In the eighteenth century, the word 'spiritual' meant everything from psychological to the paranormal, and psychology became a good word, stripped of occult overtones, only after the works of Freud and Jung in the twentieth century. In Indian thought, in Buddhist, Jain and Hindu scriptures, the spiritual was primarily about the mind, the expanding mind, that can even reach infinity.

This is why yoga in America is simply seen as an exotic form of physical exercise, with greater value given to postures (asanas) with little value given to breath (pranayama) and even less to meditation and other practices related to the mind. Any mention of infinite mind (brahmana) and there is panic, as evident from the many cases in American courts, that the yoga is religious!

This tendency to focus on the body over the mind is the reason why habits are so much valued in modern management. We want our employees to have good habits, behave like domesticated animals, coming on time, working effectively and efficiently, leaving on time, or late, when told, without complaint, for a pre-agreed non-exploitative fee, in an inclusive, diverse, secular ecosystem. And this is achieved through training and rigorous measurement and, of course, technology. Keeping everyone on the straight and narrow.

What is overlooked is the human mind. It loves to wander. It gets bored. It wants variety. It seeks excitement. It seeks validation and meaning. It gets distracted. It yearns for freedom. It can imagine alternate realities, even in the middle of a heated strategic meeting in the boardroom. It yearns for weekends, when it can live by its own rules, not the company's rules. It yearns for holidays.

We forget that the way a promoter looks at the company is very different from the way an employee looks at it. Most promoters follow their own habits and want the organizational processes to align with their habits, which are naturally 'good'. Many leaders believe everyone in the office must come on time, even if they come late. Many leaders insist that everyone works late, because they work late. Many leaders, who finish work on time, expect their followers also to be as efficient and effective. We assume that the world should be as we are. But the world is not. That is psychological diversity, different from physical and cosmetic diversity (gender, religion, sexuality, age and race) sought out by many multinationals today.

If we have a common goal and need everyone to align, how do we get our teams to run with us? How do we get everyone to collaborate if each one has a different habit? Who should change their habit—the leader, the follower? Must it be democratic vote?

Habits and rhythms and patterns of behaviour give us a sense of stability and security. When asked to change it, our body responds violently as it perceives it as a threat. So we resist change. We like the idea of growth but not at the cost of our habits, good or bad. While yes, mimicry of great leaders may be a good way to impress them and win favours; it remains in the end mimicry, inauthentic, a burden on our mind, that yearns to live by its own rules, not by the rules of others.

Unable to plan

It is said that in China they first build the highway and then the city. In India, they first build the city and then discover there is no highway. We can laugh about it, but it is rather depressing when you live in the city. But it is the reality of India. Why are Indians so?

Statements like Indians are bad planners and need to be 'educated' reeks of racism, cultural chauvinism and lack of perspective. It stems from the assumption that planning is a good thing for all. But is it? Unless we question fundamental assumptions we will never be able to go to the root cause of this behaviour. Let us not call this a problem. As soon as we call this a problem, we will evoke defensive behaviour and that is not what we want.

The tendency to look at life as a problem that needs to be solved is a very modern American concept, rooted in the saviour complex, whereby we see ourselves as Hollywood superheroes who want to save the world from problem-creating villains. It is a mindset that makes its way to various organizations, via various B-schools where American thought dominates the curriculum. In this mindset, those who do not agree there is a problem are seen in pathological terms: they are in denial!

Two extreme ideas emerged in India. One was the Buddhist notion of impermanence (anatta) and the other is the Hindu notion of permanence (atma). If the world is going to change anyway, why plan? If the world is not going to change, why plan? Thus both mindsets challenge the need to plan.

One can argue that India is no longer significantly Buddhist and most countries of the Far East and the South-East are. But these countries are also influenced by the Chinese Confucian tradition, Singapore being the best example, where the emperor is bound by the 'Mandate of Heaven' to create order in the land through rituals and processes and systems. Planning becomes essential here. The Chinese court was for centuries controlled by careful planning of a vast series of complex rituals that everyone adhered to.

The Chinese desire to plan comes from the Confucian value placed on order. The American value placed on planning comes from the Abrahamic idea of the Promised Land, or Jerusalem, the desire to create a great society, a desirable outcome, a destination, or goal.

Indian society, by contrast, was caste-based and every caste was essentially a professional guild (the politics and hierarchies notwithstanding). Everyone was expected to follow their community trade. Every community lived together, in relative isolation, mixing only in markets and during festivals. So the 'community' spirit was created not by 'common law' but by 'common tendency to isolate oneself' in one's group. Every group had its patriarch who directed everyone how to function. His plan was executed. Thus we see great planning and execution in caste-based events and institutions. A Hindu temple complex, managed by priests, is highly organized and based on careful planning. Trading communities are highly organized and plan rather well. Planning is part of the community process; it's not a virtue of being a human being. Democratic institutions destroy the community structure and expect humans to give up centuries of caste mindset.

Indians usually make great plans, but they are rarely implemented well, if at all. For execution of a plan means respecting it. In the Confucian way, respecting authority is the sign of being civilized. In the Abrahamic way, one is expected to follow the word of God if one loves God, as we see in the value placed on obedience of the Catholic Church that controlled Europe for a thousand years, and in the importance given to submission in Islam.

In India, the only authority that is respected is the authority of the clan: the guru, the elder, the patriarch, or the mother. No one else, certainly not a democratically elected leader, or a boss in a corporation who does not actually pay the salary but is actually as much as a servant (naukar) of the company as we are. In modern professional institutions, there is no clear master (malik) and this makes things even more confusing for a country that is used to working in family-owned businesses where authority is clearly located.

Everybody is India is told that God is inside you, which means everyone can be imaginative and find an 'upaay', a better way, a bypass that creates a short cut, or do a 'jugaad', work smartly. When everyone creates a short cut, when everyone is bypassing smartly, without perspective of the larger picture, it's a question of time that the blueprint collapses. And then work gets done only when the patriarch establishes authority by screaming and shouting at the last minute, which is how much of things in India gets done.

In a society with many variables—economics, political, social, educational, caste, religious—creating a blueprint that satisfies all is especially difficult. We forget that planning demands violent enforcement, suppression of voices of dissent once the plan is agreed upon. But in a country with so many minorities, it is tough to get consensus. Collaboration becomes tough and hence those who want to get things done either work at small community levels or turn dictatorial in exasperation. India's scale and diversity create complex governmental structures and departments, which rarely talk to each other. All these demand an extremely high level of patience to execute a plan.

Leader: 50 Insights from Mythology

49

Submit to regenerate

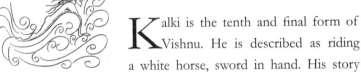 Kalki is the tenth and final form of Vishnu. He is described as riding a white horse, sword in hand. His story appears in *Vishnu Purana* around the time when Huna warlords overran the north of India somewhere in the latter part of the reign of the Gupta kings. It was elaborated over the next thousand years culminating in the *Kalki Purana* written about 500 years ago. He is often described as the avatar who is yet to come, after the Buddha. This makes him some kind of a messianic figure, a saviour, who will push back the barbarians and bring back peace and prosperity to the world.

However, this does not align well with Indian philosophy, which is based on change and rebirth. Yes, Vishnu does descend on earth from time to time, as Krishna says in the Bhagavad Gita, but not to save the world, or to get rid of villains, as is popularly believed, or even to establish justice, but to reinforce the idea of dharma. And dharma is about human potential, the human ability to help the helpless, provide resources for the meek, an idea reinforced in the first avatar of Vishnu, the fish or matsya avatar, when Vishnu takes the shape of a small fish and asks Manu, father of humanity, to save him from the big fish.

So why does Vishnu, who speaks of compassion in his first avatar, take the form of a destroyer in his final avatar? And is it the final avatar? How can there be something 'final' in a world that is described as eternal and timeless?

For that we have to understand the concept of kalpa: the lifespan of the world. Like humans, the world has a birth, a childhood, a youth, an old age and finally death. So does an idea. So does an organization. Nothing is static, everything is changing. Change demands growth in one's lifetime. Change also demands death of an old idea. Change can also demand the expansion of the mind to include a new idea.

Every world or idea or organization goes through phases. First it is fresh and new, arousing excitement. This is the Krita Yuga, the childhood innocence. Then comes the time, when it keeps its promise. When all is well. When hopes are high. This is the Treta Yuga, when Rama rules, when rules are valued. Then comes the period of decay, when survival is at stake, when the idea struggles to survive. This is the Dvapara Yuga, when hopes fade, when Krishna is needed for rules are no longer valued. Then comes the Kali Yuga, a time to withdraw from the old idea like Buddha and await the invader, Kalki, who brings new ideas. In this world view, the outsider is celebrated. He helps the insider thrive, prosper and grow by bringing in new ideas, new resources, new processes and ways of thinking.

Kalki needs to be seen differently, not as a messiah or a saviour who restores us back to the old way, but as one who brings in new ideas. And the clue lies in the horse he rides. Horses do not thrive in the Indian subcontinent and have to be continuously imported from Arabia and Central Asia via the north-west frontier. The only place they thrived was in Rajputana. The value placed on the horse in Vedic literature, and in votive offerings to brave heroes across the subcontinent, indicates the value placed on these 'imports'. For these represent fresh ideas that help in regeneration of the old.

Often organizations grow complacent with home-grown knowledge. Fat builds up. The body becomes weak and inelastic, full of self-created bureaucratic hurdles that stop it from responding to market realities. It becomes sluggish and starts losing in the market, unable to fight back, becoming prey rather than predator. To shake it up, the invader is needed—a new leader from another industry, a horde of consultants, maybe even a new investor who insists on a role in the management, any outsider who is hungry and can take advantage of the market vacuum. His arrival is violent and frightening. He shakes away the complacency, forces us to revitalize our mind and body, get rid of the fat if we have to survive. He can either invoke a competitive side in us, to fight back, or the collaborative side in us, to work together. Thus the world or idea or organization transforms. The outsider, the invader, is thus seen in a positive light, not as a destroyer of the old, but one who provokes regeneration, who helps in creating the new by reframing the old.

50

Recruitment dilemma

The Pandavas and the Kauravas were about to go to war. Both approached Krishna to help. 'Me unarmed, or my fully equipped army? Narayana or Narayani Sena?' asked Krishna. 'You,' said Arjuna, the Pandava, much to the relief of Duryodhana, the Kaurava, who was happy to get the army. What do we seek when we hire people to work for us: Narayana or Narayani Sena? Do we see who they are or do we focus only on qualifications and experience they possess? Are we the Pandavas or the Kauravas?

We would like to associate ourselves with the 'good' Pandavas and not the 'bad' Kauravas but everyone knows that management is about measurement. We cannot measure Narayana, what a person is. We can only measure Narayani, what a person has, his experience and qualifications. We hope to figure out the Narayana side during the interview process. But that remains highly subjective.

We may hear stories of great entrepreneurs who dropped out of school, who did not complete their degrees, but when it comes to recruitment, we know we want our people to be from IIT or IIM. There are at least two major FMCG firms that are very clear that marketing people have to be hired from Grade 1 B-schools and sales people may be from Grade 2 B-schools. Many consulting firms will select consultants from a set of engineering colleges and analysts from another set of engineering colleges, the assumption being that the filter used by the colleges for admission matches the filter they use for recruitment.

The primary reason for this is that the measurable Narayani is objective and justify itself in audit examination. Large-scale organizations are suspicious of subjectivity, howsoever brilliant it may be. And so Narayana is always nudged out, with greater reliance on tests and measurements. The HR team focuses on the Narayani side; the boss, who can take accountability, focuses on the Narayana side.

But recruitment needs vary for small start-ups and large steady-state organizations. The start-up needs more Narayana than Narayani as the job is unpredictable and you need people who are adaptable and highly flexible. Qualification and experience are poor indicators of the same. The steady-state organization is in a more predictable phase and so needs people who will fit into the system that is rather rigid. Here Narayani is a good enough marker.

Why would someone in a comfortable steady-state organization want to enter an unpredictable, volatile environment of a start-up? Money? Passion? If a person joins a start-up for the money, embracing the risks, he also needs to submit to the disorder that is an inevitable part of something that is being established. He also needs to have great interpersonal skills, be a leader in some situations and a follower in others, display passion, even if he may not share the entrepreneur's passion. If a person joins for passion, he also needs interpersonal skills, and the ability to either handle lack of structure, or create structure for the benefit of others. Do interviews reveal if a person has great interpersonal skills? Are we not trained to pretend by the corporate world—use the right jargon like 'team work' and 'collaboration', say what the interviewer wants to hear?

When Arjuna got Krishna, did he know what he was getting? Or was he just smitten by his friend and cousin? Did he know he would have a nervous breakdown on the brink of the war? Did he know that Krishna would sing the Bhagavad Gita? We don't know what challenges face us in the future and we only hope that those whom we recruit will have the potential to help us during unplanned, unpredicted crises. The fully equipped army of Krishna would have been of no help had Duryodhana had a nervous breakdown.

25 ▦ HarperCollins India Ltd

Celebrating 25 Years of Great Publishing

HarperCollins India celebrates its twenty-fifth anniversary in 2017. Twenty-five years of publishing India's finest writers and some of its most memorable books – those you cannot put down; ones you want to finish reading yet don't want to end; works you can read over and over again only to fall deeper in love with.

Through the years, we have published writers from the Indian subcontinent, and across the globe, including Aravind Adiga, Kiran Nagarkar, Amitav Ghosh, Jhumpa Lahiri, Manu Joseph, Anuja Chauhan, Upamanyu Chatterjee, A.P.J. Abdul Kalam, Shekhar Gupta, M.J. Akbar, Satyajit Ray, Gulzar, Surender Mohan Pathak and Anita Nair, amongst others, with approximately 200 new books every year and an active print and digital catalogue of more than 1,000 titles, across ten imprints. Publishing works of various genres including literary fiction, poetry, mind body spirit, commercial fiction, journalism, business, self-help, cinema, biographies – all with attention to quality, of the manuscript and the finished product – it comes as no surprise that we have won every major literary award including the Man Booker Prize, the Sahitya Akademi Award, the DSC Prize, the Hindu Literary Prize, the MAMI Award for Best Writing on Cinema, the National Award for Best Book on Cinema, the Crossword Book Award, and the Publisher of the Year, twice, at Publishing Next in Goa and, in 2016, at Tata Literature Live, Mumbai.

We credit our success to the people who make us who we are, and will be celebrating this anniversary with: our authors, retailers, partners, readers and colleagues at HarperCollins India. Over the years, a firm belief in our promise and our passion to deliver only the very best of the printed word has helped us become one of India's finest in publishing. Every day we endeavour to deliver bigger and better – for you.

Thank you for your continued support and patronage.

HarperCollins *Publishers* India

▼ @HarperCollinsIN

◙ @HarperCollinsIN

◘ @HarperCollinsIN

▥ HarperCollins Publishers India

www.harpercollins.co.in

Harper Broadcast

Showcasing celebrated authors, book reviews, plot trailers, cover reveals, launches and interviews, Harper Broadcast is live and available for free subscription on the brand's social media channels through a new newsletter. Hosted by renowned TV anchor and author Amrita Tripathi, Broadcast is a snapshot of all that is news, views, extracts, sneak peeks and opinions on books. Tune in to conversations with authors, where we get up close and personal about their books, why they write and what's coming up.

Harper Broadcast is the first of its kind in India, a publisher-hosted news channel for all things publishing within HarperCollins. Follow us on Twitter and YouTube.

Subscribe to the monthly newsletter here: https://harpercollins.co.in/newsletter/

▤ Harper Broadcast

▼ @harperbroadcast

www.harperbroadcast.com

Address

HarperCollins *Publishers* India Ltd
A-75, Sector 57, Noida, UP 201301, India

Phone
+91 120-4044800